Hollywood Hi·Fi

OVER **100** OF THE MOST OUTRAGEOUS CELEBRITY RECORDINGS EVER!

George Gimarc and Pat Reeder

St. Martin's Griffin
New York

Hollywood Hi·Fi

OVER 100 OF THE MOST OUTRAGEOUS
CELEBRITY RECORDINGS EVER!

Design by George Gimarc

LIBRARY OF CONGRESS CATALOGING-IN-PUBLICATION DATA

Gimarc, George.
   Hollywood hi-fi / by George Gimarc and Pat Reeder.
     p. cm.
   ISBN 0-312-14356-7
   1. Celebrities   Discography.   2. Popular music--Discography.
I. Reeder, Pat. II. Title
ML156.4.P6G56   1996   96-1698
016.78242164'0266--dc20   CIP
                                          MN

First St. Martin's Griffin Edition: May 1996
10   9 8 7 6 5 4 3 2 1

INTRODUCTION

We know what you're thinking: "An entire book about tone-deaf Hollywood actors trying to sing? WHY?" Funny you should ask!

When we first met in college, many moons ago, we realized we had something unusual in common. No, not our wickedly handsome profiles, something even rarer: an obsession with the history of pop culture that borders on lunacy, as manifested by our unwieldy collections of oddball records that the average music fan doesn't even know exist. We're talking 16 rpm radio transcription discs, obscure British punk singles, vaudeville routines on Edison cylinders, banned "party" records of the 1950s, cast LPs of Broadway musicals that closed on opening night, aircheck tapes of long-dead disc jockeys, screwy albums by such infamous eccentrics as the Shaggs, Hasil Adkins, and Wildman Fischer, and, of course, records by celebrities who are famous for anything other than their ability to sing. It's not just a morbid fascination with embarrassing incompetence; we actually *enjoy these records!* Some are truly wonderful, others so bad they're good, but we love them all. We get excited when we find a new one, and we can't wait to play it for all our friends (well, all right, for each other...we've driven away all our friends).

That's where *you* come in, New Friend! With this book, we hope to convince you that it is much more fun to laugh yourself limp at the donkey braying of that musical comedy girl, Bette Davis, than to listen to 45 minutes of C-minor arpeggios from John Tesh. At least, Bette evokes an emotional response! In this age of digital recording, when clever producers can use a host of electronic gizmos to make anyone, no matter

> "Oooh! Is Shatner going to be in it?"
> — George "Sulu" Takei

how talent-deficient (Paula Abdul, LaToya Jackson, and the Human League spring to mind), sound like a singer, it's refreshing to see stars like Clint Eastwood and Sylvester Stallone show themselves to be fallible human beings by egomaniacally insisting on recording their own amateur singing voices, warts and all. Even as we write this, Keanu Reeves and Johnny Depp are planning records with their godawful rock groups, Jerry Lewis, Rosie O'Donnell, and Brooke Shields have made their Broadway musical debuts, and Kathy Najimy is practicing a painfully off-key "Proud Mary" with her own garage band. No matter how bloodless, boring, and bland popular music becomes in the future, we know we can always count on Hollywood stars to keep serving up good old fashioned, unintentional entertainment!

Another of our goals is to provide an entertaining primer on a whole genre of records that has been largely ignored by pop culture historians. In most celebrity autobiographies, these projects rate at best a quick, embarrassed mention. We hope to rectify that sad situation, and in so doing, address some of the burning questions of our time: Why did Atlantic Records, home of the Drifters, Ray Charles, Ornette Coleman, and Erroll Garner, think it was a good idea to release a twist record by Jerry "Beaver Cleaver" Mathers? What is there about certain TV shows (*Batman, Happy Days, Star Trek, Bonanza*) that makes every single cast member think he can sing? Why do so many actors feel compelled to record with children's choruses and to cover the Rolling Stones' "Satisfaction"? The public has a right to know!

Unlike many of the singers contained herein, we would hate just to harp away on one note. So, scattered amongst the humorously hideous stuff, we have included a sampling of that rarest of all artistic creations, the truly good celebrity record. We do this in the dual hope that we can encourage more celebrities to sing, and also encourage you to spend your music dollar on something really fun by Crispin Glover or Jack Larson, rather than wasting it on vacuous "product" by Mariah Carey or Michael Bolton.

> "DON'T bE silly, REX HARRISON CAN'T SING."
> – BETTE DAVIS

Incidentally, we had no secret formula for picking the most outrageous records. We merely auditioned hundreds of candidates, then picked the ones we liked best, or that we thought would provide a good overview of this bizarre genre. We also attempted to describe, as well as print allows, just what the damn things sound like. If we left out your favorite, fret not: we're already working on Volume Two, which will include not only more movie and TV stars, but also singing writers, athletes, politicians, artists and criminals, and we welcome your input on it (see the last page for info on how to contact us).

We would like to thank some people for their help in creating this book. A tip of our fezzes to our record collector pals, especially mensch Norm Silverman, John Stainze, Doug Hanners, Dave Extram, the crowd at Record Surplus on Pico (Strike and Steve, et al.), Les Harris, David Grosblatt, Randy at RPM Records, Chuck, Lisa, and the Collector's Records gang in Dallas, and all the others who have taken our foolishly spent money. Thanks to producer Hank Levine and the many stars who graciously shared tapes and anecdotes with us. A nod of appreciation to the many authors whose books on individual stars, movies, TV shows, records, and musical theater overflow our bookshelves. Ron Lofman's "Celebrity Vocals" price guide proved to be an invaluable resource. Thanks to Digby Diehl, the Dallas Public Library, and Sims Library in Waxahachie, Texas, for research help. Gracias to our agent, David Smith, to our publicist, Jenny Owen, to Lida Ghiorzi and Bonnie Coatney for rooting for us, to Penn Jillette for making the dinner check disappear, and to Johnny Rotten for laughing at our manuscript and calling us cruel (we've never felt so proud!). Kudos to Rhino Records for defining the "Golden Throats" genre with their three fab CDs. A wiped brow of relief to Elisabeth and Paul at St. Martin's for keeping us out of trouble, and last but not least, two big, wet smooches for our wives, Donna and Laura, for inspiration and editorial advice, as well as their quiet, patient suffering.

Finally, we offer our personal guarantee to the consumer: Yes, we really have listened to each and every one of these records. All the way through. Many, many times. And paid big bucks for some of them.

Man, do we need to get a life, or what?!

> "THEY SIGNED A PETITION bEGGING ME NEVER TO SING AGAIN."
> – JOAN RIVERS

Hollywood Hi·Fi

Stars Of The Silver Scream

Bette Davis -8, Marlon Brando -11, Walter Matthau -12, Jack Lemmon -13, Gloria Swanson -14, Rock Hudson -15, Sylvester Stallone -16, Robert Mitchum -17, Mae West -18, George Burns -19, Fred MacMurray -20, Orson Welles -21, Mickey Rooney -21, Anthony Quinn -22, Telly Savalas -23, Cesar Romero -24, Fernando Lamas -24, Joe Ritchie (Joe Pesci) -25, Tippi Hedren -26, Tony Perkins -27, Ethel Merman -28

Them Hilarious Hillbillies

Petticoat Junction: Girls From Petticoat Junction -29, *Beverly Hillbillies*: Buddy Ebsen -30, Irene Ryan -31, Gomer -32, Goober -33, Dennis Weaver -34, Ken Curtis ("Festus") -35

Borscht Belters

Joan Rivers -36, Phyllis Diller -37, Buddy Hackett -38, Jack E. Leonard -39, George Jessel -40, Joe E. Ross -41

Sitcom Serenaders

Bill Cosby -42, *Hogan's Heroes* -43, Walter Brennan -44, Pepino -45, Michael McKean and David Lander -46, Laverne & Shirley -47, Barbara Feldon -48, Sally Field -49, Jackie Gleason -50, Art Carney -51, Tony Randall and Jack Klugman -52, William Frawley -53, Archie and Edith -54, Pee-Wee Herman -55

'Cause We Care So Much

Keir Dullea -56, Sissy Spacek -57, Hervé Villechaize -58

Famous Monsters & Superheroes

Ray Walston -59, Lon Chaney, Jr. -60, Boris Karloff -61, Ted Cassidy -62, Butch Patrick (Eddie & The Munsters) -63, *Batman*: Adam West and Burt Ward -64, Frank Gorshin -66, Burgess Meredith -67, Jack Larson -68

I Wanna Be A Cowboy

Goldie Hawn -69, *Bonanza* -70, Fess Parker -72, Hugh O'Brian -73, Clint Eastwood -74, Lee Marvin -75, Burt Reynolds -76

Hollywood Hi·Fi

OVER 100 OF THE MOST OUTRAGEOUS CELEBRITY RECORDINGS EVER!

Bette Davis
Two's Company
Original Cast
RCA Records LP, 1953

If we could accomplish just one thing with this book, it would be, of course, to make a great, big boatload of money. But if we could accomplish a second thing, it would be to turn a spotlight on the unjustly overlooked singing career of America's greatest screen actress, Miss Bette Davis.

Bette Davis was a glorious combination of everything we look for in an artist: a famous name from a field completely unrelated to music, an astoundingly awful singing voice, a weakness for tackling the most outlandishly inappropriate material, and the type of elephantine Hollywood ego that made her truly believe she could do anything and woe unto any peon who told her otherwise. Bette first sang in the 1943 film *Thank Your Lucky Stars* where her tongue-in-cheek rendition of "They're Either Too Young Or Too Old" failed to spark riots. Taking this as a positive sign, over the next three decades, Bette released a number of jaw-dropping singles, promoted them to no avail by singing on TV variety shows, and even made two wildly quixotic runs at Broadway musical stardom.

A typical single is "Mother Of The Bride," the bone-chilling 1965 ballad in which Mother Goddamn wails and sobs like a crazed banshee as her little girl walks down the aisle (the groom will be lucky if he doesn't end up buried alive in his mother-in-law's basement). The flip side is a gooey, Rod McKuen-style poem, again wildly overacted to orchestral accompaniment. It's called "Life Is A Lonely Thing," and you will be, too, if you play it for your friends. "Single" (Mercury, 1965) was an answer record to Richard Burton's song, "Married Man," in which Bette answered Burton's singing success in *Camelot* by singing *a lot* like a camel. We must also mention Bette's 1962 mondo-bizarro attempt at a twist hit "Whatever Happened To Baby Jane?" which is even funnier than watching Joan Crawford eat rats. After this release, Bette quite reasonably decided that she was born to sing horror themes, and was miffed when the studio refused to let her sing the theme to *Hush, Hush, Sweet Charlotte* (1965), opting instead for Al Martino. Bette believed she could easily have outsold Patti Page's hit version, if only they had let her record it with the Brothers Four. She declared, "They haven't had a hit in a long time, and if they could have done 'Charlotte' with me, it would have been the biggest hit IN THE WORLD!" Bette Davis always insisted that her bizarre singles would be massive hits, although none ever were. To find out why, pick up the compilation LP *Bette Davis Sings* (Citadel, 1985). It is highly recommended for Davis fans, drag queens, or anyone who is seeking a nonchemical way to peel paint.

Still, when it comes time to pick the most outrageous Bette Davis record of them all, there is no contest: it has to be the justly obscure original cast LP of *Two's Company*, Bette's first ill-fated stab at becoming a Broadway musical star.

Two's Company was a weak sketch-comedy revue with undistinguished songs by Ogden Nash, Sammy Cahn, and Vernon Duke. Ignoring her many advisors' warnings, Bette agreed to do it because she hoped to show the world she had talents beyond being the grande dame of cinematic bitchery: "The New Bette Davis! She yodels! She jumps about to music!" The show spent several rocky months on the road, during which the cast and crew quickly grew to hate Bette and her entourage, then opened on Broadway on December 15, 1952. Despite scathing reviews, the theaters in every town were always standing-room-only, thanks to an army of rabid Bette Davis worshipers who would have gladly paid to watch their idol recite the alphabet with a mouth full of chewing tobacco. In fact, that might have been preferable to what she offered them in *Two's Company*.

Vernon Duke later said of his beloved ingenue, "Bette had four notes to her voice, all of them bad," and he wasn't kidding. From her very first track on this LP, "Turn Me Loose On Broadway," you know you're in for a bumpy night indeed, as Miss Davis galumphs about the stage with the chorus boys, declaring that she's finally found her true calling as a "musical comedy girl!" Combining the same clipped delivery that she brought to her classic line "WHAT-a-DUMP!" with a singing voice that sounds like a rusty Klaxon horn, Bette demands, "Give me some JOKES, and a CORN-ee rou-TINE! GIVE me a POP-u-lah TUNE!...To!...WAH!-BUHL!" It appears that turning Bette Davis loose on Broadway was roughly equivalent to turning a cougar loose on a hamster! We can just imagine the first-nighters staring at the spectacle with their mouths agape, like the audience at "Springtime for Hitler" in *The Producers*.

Ah, but there's much, much more! Like "Roll Along, Sadie," a production number featuring Bette as Somerset Maugham's famous prostitute, Sadie Thompson, who drives men insane, probably by singing to them in bed. We defy you to listen to this cut without picturing her in a pinafore, dementedly honking, "I've written a lettah to Dah-dee..." (One critic claimed that Bette in her Sadie getup reminded him of a female impersonator.) Or needle drop on the song "Purple Rose," an ersatz hillbilly hoedown which Bette yowled through comical, blacked-out front teeth, like Lucille Ball with a bad attitude... except compared to Bette's painfully off-key hollering, the gravel-voiced Lucy was Patsy Cline. Yet all this is merely a prelude to the piéce-de-résistance: Bette's heart- and ear-wrenching ballad, "Just Like A Man" (see: "*Joan Rivers*"). One of the dancers recalled that when Bette was good on this song, she was terrific, but when she was bad, it was so embarrassing, the rest of the cast would just sneak out of the theater. This album must have been recorded on a sneaker night: as Bette croaks her way through this curtain-

closer, which is both a third-rate torch song and a parody of a third-rate torch song, we swear you can actually *hear* every last cigarette she ever chain-smoked!

New York Times critic Walter Kerr assessed Bette's musical debut quite succinctly when he wrote, "It's a lot like listening to Beethoven's Fifth played on a pocket comb. You marvel that it can be done at all. And five minutes is just about enough of it." Horrid as it was, the show was usually sold out, thanks mostly to Bette's loyal gay fans keeping it open. (She reportedly repaid them by privately griping about the theater always being packed with "fags," including a ten-year-old boy whose mother Bette felt was warping him into a pervert by indulging his interest in musicals.) After ninety performances, *Two's Company* abruptly closed when Bette became sick from an infected tooth...although rumors flew that she faked her illness to escape the awful reviews, made even worse by the raves for the musical debut of her Tinseltown rival, Rosalind Russell, in *Wonderful Town*. The *Two's Company* cast album was cut one year later, and true to form, Bette never even considered that its low sales had anything to do with her singing. Instead, she blamed its failure on the fact that there just wasn't enough of *her* on it! We heartily agree, yet even with a scant five cuts to her credit, this LP remains a true Hollywood Hi-Fi classic. If William Shatner's *Transformed Man* is the Holy Grail of Bad Celebrity Singing, then *Two's Company* is the Holy Grailette!

In 1974, Bette took another lunge at Broadway, this time with *Miss Moffat*, a musical version of her 1945 film, *The Corn Is Green*. Producer Joshua Logan, who had worked on *Two's Company* and really should have known better, hired Bette in hopes that she would "act" her songs, as Rex Harrison had in *My Fair Lady*. Unfortunately, Bette still believed that she could sing and insisted on doing so. According to biographer James Spada, during one rehearsal, her understudy tried to compliment her by saying that she had done a song "just like Rex Harrison," and Bette snapped, "Don't be silly! Rex Harrison can't sing!" She also couldn't remember her lines or lyrics, at one performance turning to the orchestra leader in mid-song and demanding, "Where the hell am I?" Fifteen shows into a scheduled forty-four-week tryout tour, Bette dropped out, pleading back pain, but it couldn't have been worse than the ear pain the rest of the cast was suffering. Logan had shrewdly taken out insurance against her departure, but tragically, no cast LP was ever recorded. Connoisseurs of humiliating musical performances by legendary Hollywood divas can only fasten their seat belts, drop on *Two's Company*, and imagine the wonderful entertainment they missed!

Marlon Brando
Guys And Dolls soundtrack
Decca Records LP, 1955

Funny how a little bad timing at one point in history can be the curse of all posterity. In 1955, Hollywood was planning a movie of *Guys And Dolls*. The hit Broadway show was based on Damon Runyon's stories about footloose gamblers and was blessed with one of the all-time great scores by Frank Loesser. So who better to play swingin', singin' high-roller Sky Masterson than Frank Sinatra? Would you believe...Marlon Brando?! At the time, Brando was Hollywood's hottest star, so MGM tapped the future Godfather for his first musical. Brando warned director Joe Mankiewicz that he couldn't sing, but Mankiewicz blithely replied that he'd never directed a musical before, so they would just learn together. After two weeks' practice with a voice coach, Brando entered the recording studio. But he later admitted that he still "couldn't hit a note with a baseball bat," and his songs had to be assembled note by note from dozens of attempts. He's not horrible, but his thin, nasal tenor does suggest a comedian doing a singing Brando impression in a *Forbidden Broadway* sketch. He also complained that the notes were edited so tightly together, he almost asphyxiated himself lip-synching to them, because he had no time to breathe between lines.

But what really made this one of the all-time masterpieces of miscasting is that Frank Sinatra was actually *in* the movie...in the second lead of Nathan Detroit...you know, the part *without* the good songs! One can only imagine the thoughts of the crew as they filmed Brando mumbling "Luck Be A Lady" (released as a single, for swooning bobby-soxers), while over in the corner, awaiting his next nonmusical scene, Frank Sinatra sat munching doughnuts and reading *Variety*. In 1994, this film made headlines again when Barbra Streisand's concert tour resurrected it and actually charged fans $350 each to hear Marlon sing. As a teenager, Babs was smitten by the warbling Wild One, and she watched *Guys And Dolls* over and over at a Brooklyn theater. Since her concert was scripted as a look back at her life during a visit to her psychiatrist, she dragged her early Brando fixation out of her psyche, put a clip of him singing "I'll Know" on a huge video screen, and played out her fantasy of being Jean Simmons (Brando's lovely costar, *not* the bass player for KISS) by singing a duet with the crooning Corleone. She then told her psychiatrist what an inspiring singer Brando was, which provided a perfect segue into her title role in *Nuts*. Of course, today, anyone can buy this LP or rent *Guys And Dolls* on video. And like Streisand, you, too, can sit transfixed as Marlon Brando struggles stiffly through this terrific, swingin' score, while Sinatra stands idly by, taking pointers on his diction and planning his next LP, *Songs For Mumblin' Lovers*.

Walter Matthau
"Bring Her Back To Me"
Columbia Records 45, 1965

Nineteen sixty-five was a milestone year for Walter Matthau. Despite dozens of fine performances in movies and plays, his Average Joe looks had made little impression on the public. He appeared to be destined for a lifetime of unrewarding character roles. Then he starred opposite Art Carney in Neil Simon's 1965 Broadway smash *The Odd Couple*. Overnight, he became America's favorite comic slob, the curmudgeonly, cigar-chomping, beer-swilling Oscar Madison, and the offers started pouring in. Fortunately for us, one of those offers was to record a single for Columbia Records.

"Bring Her Back To Me" is the type of cornball, 1890s-style tearjerker you would expect from George Jessel, but it was turned into a hilarious spoof, purely by Matthau's performance. It starts with a male chorus that sounds like a barbershop quartet of Dudley Do-Right clones singing in perfect harmony, "If you find her, bring her back to me." A plaintive harmonica warbles, as Matthau begins reciting the verse in a thick-tongued, drunken slur that is so brilliantly authentic, it took ten close listenings to decide that he (probably) wasn't really soused. Matthau portrays a repentant father who buttonholes a cop ("Shay, offisher...") and tearfully moans that he is searching the streets for his daughter, whom he cruelly tossed out when she got in trouble with a man. So far, it's moderately amusing, but nothing special. Then, we arrive at the refrain. Fasten your seat belts, kids: Walter Matthau is about to sing!

As the deadpan chorus hums flawlessly behind him, Matthau suddenly lets fly with a sound that can only be likened to a bloodhound baying madly at the full moon. He is so far from the melody, he's in a different time zone! "Brrrrrrring 'errr baaaaaAAAack! Where she beloooOOooOOOoooOOOngs!... EEeeeEEeeeeEEEf you fiiiiiiiillllliiind 'er, Hmmmmbriiiiing 'er baaaAAAaaack t'meeee!!" His bellowing is breathtakingly ghastly, yet wonderfully unself-conscious; it's as if he's singing at the top of his lungs in the shower and thinks nobody can hear him...or if they can, he just doesn't give a damn! We've heard this record dozens of times, and it always leaves us limp with laughter. We anoint it a four-star Hollywood Hi-Fi classic!

Tragically, Matthau made very few records, because his bad experience shooting *Hello, Dolly* (1969) with Barbra Streisand forever soured him on musicals. Babs reportedly felt insecure because she was horribly miscast, and this made her even more of an on-set tyrant than usual. Matthau finally blew up and told her off, which resulted in her giving him the nickname "Old Sewer-mouth." He, in turn, gifted her with the affectionate appellation "Miss Ptomaine." Later, he said he would work with her again only in "something appropriate. Perhaps *Macbeth*." Say, how about a musical version?

Jack Lemmon
A Twist of Lemmon
Epic Records LP, 1958

Jack Lemmon is one of America's most beloved actors (Shirley MacLaine once declared him "the nicest man in Hollywood") as well as one of the most versatile (he handles comedy and drama with equal aplomb). But you might not be aware that he is also a talented pianist whose earliest ambition was not to act, but to become the next George Gershwin.

Jack Lemmon taught himself to play piano by ear at age thirteen, and entertained classmates with Tin Pan Alley tunes and his own compositions. At Harvard, he wrote the musical score for the 1945 Hasty Pudding Club show, including a romantic ditty entitled "The Bottom's Fallen Out Of Everything But You." While struggling to make it on Broadway, he supported himself as a saloon pianist. He wrote the scores for a Broadway musical that was never seen (he claims that two days before the out-of-town opening, the producer was hauled away in a straitjacket) and for his 1957 film, *Fire Down Below* (after four years, his publishing royalty check totaled $17). And of course, he made his greatest contribution to music by donning a gorilla suit and playing a member of Ernie Kovacs' robotic, simian samba band, the Nairobi Trio.

But Lemmon's musical talents first became known to the public at large in 1958, with the release of his first LP, *A Twist of Lemmon*. He originally planned it to be all piano and orchestra instrumental versions of his own tunes ("With All My Love") and various standards ("Bidin' My Time," "Let's Fall In Love"). But much to his later regret, he let Epic honcho Joe Sherman convince him to make it four instrumentals...and eight vocals!

Lemmon's ivory-tickling is impressive, but it is impossible to hear him sing without visualizing a typical scene from one of his early movies: brash but naive young Madison Avenue ad man is preparing for a date with reputedly hot-to-trot secretary (Shirley MacLaine). Wearing only a towel around his waist, he splashes on Canoe aftershave, practices seductive tango glances in the bathroom mirror, and excitedly sings to himself, "It wuzzz the kisssss...heard rrrround...the wuuuh-urld! Ya-de-da-de-dah! Tee-hee!!" Lemmon later joked that he knew only four people who bought this LP. He believed it failed because he relied too much on his movie persona, and vowed that if he ever recorded again, he would simply play the music of great composers. After blessing us with more vocals on a collection of 1920s oldies (*Jack Lemmon Sings and Plays Music from Some Like It Hot*, Columbia, 1959), he kept his vow in 1972, when he surprised many fans, and won an Emmy by hosting the television special "Jack Lemmon in 'S Wonderful, 'S Marvelous, 'S Gershwin" (soundtrack LP on Daybreak). He still sings occasionally, on records and talk shows, and you can hear him warble in the 1955 musical *My Sister Eileen.* But none of those performances came with the subtle warning that was displayed on the cover of his first LP: a lovely bowl, filled to overflowing with lemons.

Gloria Swanson
Boulevard!
BLD:GS Records LP, 1979

I'M STILL BIG— IT'S THE PICTURES THAT GOT SMALLER!

GLORIA **SWANSON** IN **BOULEVARD!**

THE LONG AWAITED MUSICAL ADAPTATION OF *SUNSET BOULEVARD*

VOCAL SELECTIONS INCLUDE
STAY CLOSE
THERE'S AN ANGLE
I'M A NATIVE
WHAT'S THE ANSWER?
TALK! TALK! TALK!
OFF WITH THE OLD
THOSE WONDERFUL PEOPLE
HAND IT TO THE GLANDS

Long before Andrew Lloyd Webber turned Billy Wilder's classic 1950 film, *Sunset Boulevard*, into an overstuffed, half-baked Puccini zucchini, there was an initial attempt at musicalizing the property. And the mad genius behind it was none other than Miss Norma Desmond herself, Gloria Swanson. Her success can be surmised by noting that in her 535-page autobiography, Swanson managed to discuss everything from her abortion to the curative powers of vegetarianism, yet never once mentioned *Boulevard!* the musical.

Shortly after making her Oscar-nominated comeback as the deranged silent film star in *Sunset Boulevard*, Swanson realized that her success was a mixed blessing: she was in demand again, but all the parts she was offered were Norma Desmond clones. Figuring that if she had to play the same role forever, she might as well do something new with it, she hit on the idea of a Broadway musical version. In 1955, she received tentative approval from Paramount, then spent two years and a pile of her own money developing the project. Eerily prescient, she hired a couple of Brits, Dickson Hughes and Richard Stapley, to write the show, and planned to open it first in London, then spring it on America.

Working with Swanson, the pair made some bizarre plot changes that would clearly have ruined Wilder's dark satire of Hollywood. For instance, the film's famous, tragic finale was to be replaced by a happy ending. Accounts differ, but it was either to end with the gigolo screenwriter Joe falling in love with Norma, instead of being shot by her, or else with Norma giving her blessing to Joe and his new, young girlfriend (and which of those scenarios strikes you as less likely?). At least they ruled out killing Joe then bringing him back to life with vegetarianism. No wonder Erich von Stroheim turned down an offer to play Max the chauffeur again, opting instead to die.

In 1957, just as Swanson was preparing to stage the show, Paramount decided that it would undermine future re-releases of the movie, and yanked the rights. All that survives from the debacle is this obscure LP, which sounds like a backers' audition in someone's living room, accompanied by an upright piano. The singing is okay when you can hear it, but half the time the performers are either turned away from the lone microphone or tripping over the furniture. The songs are, at best, uninspired. A typical example: a patter song called "Hand It To The Glands." This is what they'll be humming as they walk up the aisle, eh? If only they'd thought to rip off Puccini!

This is more of an archaeological artifact than a cast album. But if you are a struggling theater company that can't pay those stiff Andrew Lloyd Webber royalties, then please note that the entire score of *Boulevard!* is reportedly gathering dust somewhere in the Gloria Swanson Collection at the University of Texas. Break a leg!

Rock Hudson
"Pillow Talk"
Decca Records 45, 1959

Hollywood is a factory town whose only product is illusions, and during the 1950s, its two most amazing illusions were that Rock Hudson was heterosexual and Doris Day was a virgin.

The truth about these costars was well known to insiders (Groucho Marx once said that he was so old, he knew Doris Day before she was a virgin), but that did not prevent the studios from going to great lengths to maintain their squeaky-clean public images. Herculean efforts were expended to protect Hudson's macho veneer, including fake-dates with comely starlets, publicity photos of Rock engaged in manly activities, and an arranged marriage to his press agent's secretary. And in a display of discretion unimaginable in the *Geraldo* era, his fellow actors voluntarily kept Rock's secret for years, out of respect for a talented actor who was considered one of the kindest and most generous men in town.

This record is a shining example of those herculean efforts. The theme song from the hit comedy *Pillow Talk*, it was sung in the movie by Doris Day, a former band singer (imagine one of those being a virgin!). But the studio must have realized that these lyrics were perfect for reinforcing Rock's heart-throb image, so the nonsinging stud was hustled out of the leather bars and into the recording studio posthaste. Rock actually acquits himself nicely as a singer, but the record is hilarious today for its perfect, hermetically-sealed portrait of the square-jawed *Playboy* man of 1959: secure in his masculinity, happy in his footloose bachelorhood, yet still hopeful that somewhere out there, "there must be a pillow-talkin' girl for me!" The bouncy tune includes accompaniment by the Rhythmaires, who offer swingin' "dooba-dooba-dooo's," and at one point lament, "All he does is talk, talk to his pillow!" Yeah, like Rock Hudson was sleeping alone because he just couldn't find the right girl! Their presence makes this record sound even more like a Stan Freberg parody. Still, we're sure that many deluded female fans bought it, sighed over it, and slept with the picture sleeve on their very own pillows. If they'd only known!

If you're really Rock crazy, you'll also want to check out the 1955 soap opera *All That Heaven Allows*, in which the manly gardener played by Rock Hudson tickles the ivories and melts reluctant rich widow Jane Wyman with a light pillow-talky tune. Scared off the music scene for a little over a decade, Rock recorded an entire album of ballads (*Rock Gently*, 1971) on Rod McKuen's Stanyan Records label at the same time he was starring in *McMillan And Wife*. Unfortunately, fan's hopes for an LP of duets with Jim Nabors proved futile.

Sylvester Stallone
"Too Close To Paradise"
Paradise Alley soundtrack
MCA Records LP, 1978

It may be hard for you youngsters to believe, but once upon a time, a Sylvester Stallone movie won the Academy Award for Best Picture! No, we ain't a-funnin' ya: it was the original *Rocky*, and it came out of nowhere to earn critical acclaim and tons of money, turning its unknown writer/star into a Hollywood power virtually overnight. But one thing seemed to grate on Sly: he felt that if only he, and not Oscar-winning Best Director John Avildsen, had directed the picture, then it might have been *really* successful.

So it wasn't surprising that once Sly got the juice to make a picture *his* way, it was more than a vanity project: it was a vanity project on steroids. Stallone wrote a script called *Paradise Alley*, about three brothers fighting their way out of poverty. (Ha! Fooled you! It's about wrestling, not boxing!) He directed it. He starred in it, as "The Brother With The Most Dialogue." He wrote a novelization of his brilliant screenplay. And naturally he had to sing the theme song, too! "Too Close To Paradise" is an overwrought, "gonna believe in myself and climb that mountain" style ballad, the kind Michael Bolton has made a career out of inflicting on us. As usual, it starts out soft and pensive, then quickly builds to an endless series of noisy crescendos, drenched with swirling strings, crashing cymbals, and a frenzied gospel choir, as all the musicians and singers work themselves into a lather over how much too close to paradise they all are. And in the eye of this hurricane stands that pumped-up soul man, Sylvester Stallone! Sly croons! He moans! He gets carried away and testifies, "I can't stand it out on da street no mo'! Oh God, it's cold!" Rather than buying a sweater, he attempts one of those ascending, Whitney Houston wails ("I'm too close to Par-ah-dieeiiieeeiiiiise!") and sounds like he's practicing for his diving-off-a-mountain scene in *Cliffhanger*, or perhaps a remake of *Tarzan*. Sly's note-bending skills make Bruce Willis sound like Luther Vandross. The first thing his singing voice calls to mind is a cross between the mating cry of the bull moose and the older, drugged-out Elvis after a long day in the dentist's chair. No wonder he decided after this to leave his soundtracks to real singing talents, like his brother, Frank.

Incidentally, we chose this over the equally worthy soundtrack of *Rhinestone* (the only movie where Dolly Parton's costar has a bigger chest than she does) for three reasons: 1) It's much more obscure and deserves exposure; 2) in *Rhinestone*, Sly was *supposed* to be playing a bad singer, so it could be his least challenging role ever; 3) Sly was paid $5 million to sing in *Rhinestone*. For $5 million, we'd sing Gilbert & Sullivan naked in the lobby of Trump Tower. But the embarrassing debacle of "Too Close To Paradise" was all Stallone's idea, and he practically begged for all the credit, even to the point of stickering the LP jacket...so we're happy to give it to him!

Robert Mitchum
Calypso...Is Like So...
Capitol Records LP, 1957

Robert Mitchum has held more jobs than any actor in history. Not temperamentally suited for waiting tables ("Hi, I'm Robby, your waiter. Hurry up and order before I slug ya one"), Mitchum's initial career choice was teen hobo. Arrested for vagrancy, he spent a week on a Georgia chain gang before fleeing west in a hail of bullets. He then worked as a dishwasher, nightclub bouncer, engine wiper on a freighter, ghostwriter for a celebrity astrologer, drop-hammer operator at Lockheed, and poet, among other jobs. Even after achieving stardom, he still dabbled in other professions, such as jailbird (fifty-nine days for possession of pot in 1949). But would you believe calypso musician? Isn't that Louis Farrakhan's territory?

The helpful liner notes attempt to assuage our shock: "Surprised that Robert Mitchum sings calypso? It would be stranger if he couldn't!" While neglecting to mention his familiarity with ganja, the notes inform us that Mitchum developed a love for calypso while filming in Trinidad, and tried to interest his Hollywood pals in the island sound. Capitol Records, impressed by Mitchum's "authentic flavor, beat, and vitality" (and perhaps also impressed by the way he refused to squeal on other Hollywood pot-puffers in 1949), insisted that he record the songs himself. It didn't hurt that at the time, Harry Belafonte ruled the record charts, Trader Vic's was doing a booming business in phosphorescent rum drinks served in plastic coconut shells, and Americans seemed willing to buy anything with bongos on it.

So, how good does Robby Mitchum do de calypso, mon? Well, he's a more authentic calypso singer than Vanilla Ice was a rapper. He does a decent job on the tongue-twisting lyrics, especially on the up-tempo "What's This Generation Coming To?" a lament about how da crazy teenagers got da nation in a state of con-fyoo-shun wit' dere rockin' 'n' rollin'. A Capitol trade-paper ad breathlessly declared that this cut, b/w "Mama, Looka Boo Boo," had been *RUSH*-released as a single "because of its powerful hit potential." (It wasn't a hit, although it is kinda catchy.) On other tunes, his vocals (sorry, his "virile pipes") aren't as powerful as his fists, but as Johnny Mercer once said, if Mitchum can't reach a high note, "he can act his way through it." And if that doesn't work...well, who's gonna *tell* him?

We can truthfully say that if you're aching to hear Robert Mitchum sing calypso songs, this is definitely the LP to own. That's because sales were so tepid, Mitchum never recorded another calypso album. However, in 1958, he cowrote and recorded the immensely popular "Ballad of Thunder Road," which in turn inspired one of the best songs of Bruce Springsteen's Early Non-Whiny Period. We shudder to think what The Boss might sound like today if he had purchased "Calypso Is Like So" instead! Tramps like us, baby, we were born to limbo!!!

Mae West
Great Balls Of Fire
MGM Records LP, 1972

Mae West
"Great Balls Of Fire"

It sounds like the perfect match: the woman who corrupted America's morals in the 1930s sings the rock ditties that corrupted America's morals in the 1950s and 1960s. Mae's sexy double entendres and risqué songs like "I Wonder Where My Easy Rider's Gone?" got her arrested for obscenity and helped bring on the creation of the censorious Hayes office. Mae was to the morality of the thirties what Madonna was to the eighties. So why do we end up laughing at her rock 'n' roll singing and shuddering at the jokes?

The problem is, by the time Mae West got around to making a rock album, she was eighty years old! Still, her mummified state seems to have made her no less horny, judging by the revamped lyrics of the rock classics on this album. "Great Balls Of Fire" makes Jerry Lee Lewis look downright subtle, as our Mae makes it disturbingly clear that the "great balls of fire" she is growling about are not Bill Haley's Comets, but appendages on a sweaty muscle-man. "Happy Birthday Sweet 16" becomes "Happy Birthday Sweet 21," as Mae creepily seduces a fan who first wrote to her when he was nine, but now that he's twenty-one, it's legal for her to give him much more than an autograph (*Harold And Maude* fans take note). And in "Rock Around The Clock," Mae warns her winded lover that "when the clock strikes two, three, and four, if you go slow, I'll yell for more."

Besides the desecration of rock 'n' roll classics, there's also a handful of smutty, witless original tunes which are closer to the leering Benny Hill than the classic camp of Mae West. They include "How Miss West Won World Peace," in which Mae does her bit to relieve international tensions by nailing every diplomat at the U.N. She is accompanied by a sleazy sax that makes it sound as if she's about to strip (NOOOOO!!!).

Having celebrated the anniversary of her own "Sweet 16" party sixty-four times, Mae's voice is even thinner than it used to be. She still punctuates every song with her patented orgasmic grunts, but that could be arthritis pains. Ironically, the only moment of restraint comes on the Doors' "Light My Fire," when someone sensitive to Mae's mortality changed the lyric from "and our love becomes a funeral pyre" to "flaming pyre," for obvious reasons. Even so, Mae's Poli-Grip pronunciation renders the inflammatory phrase as "our love becomes a flaming pie."

If you enjoy this LP, you will also enjoy necrophilia. Plus, check out Mae's last film, *Sextette* (1978), in which several misguided rock stars fought for the chance to feign lust for the octogenarian ingenue (playing a girl of twenty-five!). Among them, Keith Moon, Ringo Starr, and a nearly unrecognizable Alice Cooper, singing a disco number that almost killed his career.

Other recordings: Tons of them, but the earlier, the better.

George Burns
George Burns Sings
Buddah Records LP, 1969

In his heartwarming memoir, *Gracie: A Love Story,* George Burns fondly recalls the Cherry Sisters, a vaudeville act whose entire claim to fame was that they were the worst singers in the world. They would come out onstage, a safety net would be lowered to protect them, they would start to sing, and audiences would hurl fruit at them.

Something about this act must've impressed Burns (perhaps the extra money the sisters made by selling fruit in the lobby), because he turned his own bad singing into a running gag. While insisting on singing at parties, he would seldom do an entire song on radio or TV. Instead, he would zip through a couple of lines of some old chestnut in his patented, triple-time monotone, then be interrupted by a caustic joke about his bad voice. So, naturally, when Neil Bogart offered him a chance to do an album for Buddah, Burns assumed it would be a comedy record.

Much to Burns's trepidation, Bogart and producer Lewis Merenstein had in mind a serious musical LP in which Burns would, for the first time, sing ballads all the way through at the right tempo. Burns agreed, on condition that he could also record comedy bits to put between the songs. But the songs turned out so good, the comedy bits were shelved.

The only humor comes from a few of the song lyrics ("I Kissed Her On The Back Porch"), Burns's one lapse into triple-time mumbling ("It All Depends On You"), and the cover, which in the original release spoofed the Beatles' *Sgt. Pepper* album, with Burns in love beads standing in front of a group of all his showbiz pals, from Jack Benny to Jerry Lewis. The *Sgt. Pepper* theme is also echoed by the first cut, "With A Little Help From My Friends" (Burns is easing into singing gradually; he must've figured that even he could sing better than Ringo Starr). From then on, you're hooked.

When George Burns sings about old age in "Mr. Bojangles" and "Old Folks," all other singers suddenly sound like five-year-olds (except Paula Abdul, who *always* sounds like a five-year-old.) The cuts include nostalgic standards ("Ain't Misbehavin'," "You Made Me Love You"), vaudeville tunes ("Grizzly Bear"), and a few well-chosen sixties pop tunes ("King Of The Road," Harry Nilsson's "1941"). The only semi-clinker is "Satisfaction," but it's still better than Phyllis Diller's version. Overall, this is a gem of an album that not only surprised Burns's fans, it surprised George as well. The LP launched him on a new career as a singer at seventy-three, and was followed by such hits as "I Wish I Was Eighteen Again" (1980) and "Young At Heart" (1982). Combine that with his new career as a movie star, launched by the Oscar he won for *The Sunshine Boys* at seventy-nine, and you have a pretty powerful argument against mandatory retirement laws.

Forget what you've heard: Clapton's not God. George Burns is God!

Fred MacMurray
"The Flubber Song"
Buena Vista Records 45, 1962

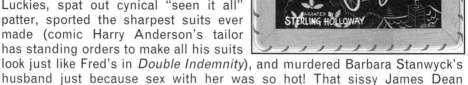

We would like to posit a startling theory: Fred MacMurray was the coolest star in Hollywood! Ponder the following dramatic evidence.

1. Fred MacMurray starred in the coolest film noir ever, *Double Indemnity*, in which he sucked down bourbon and Luckies, spat out cynical "seen it all" patter, sported the sharpest suits ever made (comic Harry Anderson's tailor has standing orders to make all his suits look just like Fred's in *Double Indemnity*), and murdered Barbara Stanwyck's husband just because sex with her was so hot! That sissy James Dean would've just sat around sniveling!

2. He played the world's coolest musical instrument, the sax, but never yielded to the temptation to release a bad celebrity album of saxophone instrumentals!

3. He once replied to one of the authors' childhood fan letters with an autographed photo, *personally* inscribed, not stamped by a machine or forged by an underling. It took a year to arrive, but it was worth the wait!

4. Sure, *My Three Sons* was incredibly lame. But Fred was so cool, he forced the producers to let him come in just once a week and shoot all his scenes at once, thereby never having to rub elbows with the odious Dodie or the creepy confirmed bachelor *Uncle* Charley!

5. Fred MacMurray invented Flubber, making absentminded professors cool and boosting the self-esteem of millions of science nerds! Which leads us to this record, a nifty slice of "Monster Mash"-style novelty rock, in which a trio of bubbleheaded, but no doubt babe-a-licious, coeds inquire about the Professor's ginchy new invention. (What college professor, other than the one on "Gilligan's Island," had his own cheerleaders?!) He informs them, with gleeful "mad scientist" abandon, that Flubber is "the greatest! It's a boon to man!" As the weird "Flub-a-dubba-dubba" sound effects roll in and out, the wide-eyed chickies chant, "If nothing else can doooo it..." and Fred ripostes, "A-ha!! FLUBBER CAN!!!" The track even includes a hot, honkin' sax solo in the Bill Haley mold. Could it be Fred himself? Doubtful, but we can dream, can't we? This song didn't appear in the movie and was only released as a kiddie single and as a track on the Disney album pictured above, featuring Sterling Holloway telling the story of "The Absent Minded Professor." But this cut is way too cool to waste on rug rats. In fact, if there were any true justice in this world, the song would be covered by that other great Fred in the B-52s immediately!

Spin this deliriously giddy platter a few times, then rent *Double Indemnity* or *Murder, He Says.* Soon, you too will be shouting, "Never mind the Dead Heads! I'm a Fred Head!"

Orson Welles
"I Know What It Is
  To Be Young"
GNP Records 45, 1984

Mickey Rooney
"Lover Of
  The Simple Things"
New Horizons 45, 1984

There is an unwritten law in Hollywood that if an actor can survive booze, flops, scandals, divorces, and all other pitfalls of stardom, and reach the age of sixty-five alive and still reasonably famous, then he gets to record a mawkish ballad about his philosophy of life. And so, on these 45s, two aging movie giants share with us the wisdom they've acquired during their autumnal years of doing wine commercials and road shows of *Sugar Babies*.

As you might expect, Orson Welles's record is the heavier of the two: the sleeve declares it "The Song For All Seasons!... A once-in-a-lifetime recording that could well become a collector's item," much like "Precious Moments" decorative figurines and Elvis commemorative plates. "I Know What It Is To Be Young, (But You Don't Know What It Is To Be Old)" is a violin-drenched, minor-key, Charles Aznavour-ish ballad in which the weepy Ray Charles Singers gush that their lives have been changed forever by the words of an old man (Welles), who then rumblingly recites his mystical wisdom. This includes the following: young people don't think about age as much as old people do...young and old people should get together more often...and winter follows summer. Wow! You can find more advice from Welles on his only other recording, the narrative he did for his daughter's favorite metal band Manowar, on their 1982 LP "Battle Hymns."

If your life isn't changed yet, try **Mickey Rooney's** "Lover Of The Simple Things," which was recorded in Las Vegas, as you can tell from the bluesy, "Quarter To Three" backing track and from Mick's chuckling, saloon-singer asides. ("That's just the way it is, baby! Heh-heh! Gotta take it, mama!"). He's a regular Mickey Rat Pack. His voice has more gravel than the Nevada desert, but at least he does sing, and on key, too! Mick's tips for a full life include: Take time for both work and play... stop to smell the flowers... and don't worry about money, or as he puts it, "I wouldn't chase a fortune 'round the corner." Smart advice coming from a man who chased every skirt 'round the corner until he had to declare bankruptcy in 1962 after blowing most of his twelve-million-dollar fortune on alimony payments.

It's hard to believe this is all the wisdom these men have to offer. Both were multi-talented child prodigies. Welles cowrote, directed, and starred in the greatest film in history, *Citizen Kane* (1941), while Rooney was the top box office star in America at nineteen. Between the two of them, they had eleven wives, including Ava Gardner (Rooney) and Rita Hayworth (Welles). And all they have to say is "Stop and smell the roses"?! We could get that from Mac Davis! Come on, guys: at least tell us how to pick up women! It's no wonder all the good songs about getting old go to George Burns.

Anthony Quinn
In My Own Way...I Love You
Capitol Records LP, 1969

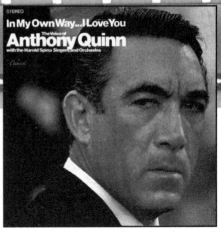

Born in Mexico of Irish and Mexican parents, Anthony Quinn easily became Hollywood's favorite "one size fits all" Swarthy Foreigner. This veritable one-man Rainbow Coalition has played everything from Mexican banditos to Arab sultans to Italian mafia dons. But thanks to his great success in *Zorba The Greek* (1964), most people think of him as a boisterous, Grecian force of nature, a brute of a fellow who nevertheless can teach us uptight Americanos a thing or two about the joys of sex, booze, and living life to the fullest.

So it seemed only natural to take Anthony Quinn into a recording studio and let him ruminate on love's mysteries, to the romantic accompaniment of the Harold Spina Singers and Orchestra. As album producer Spina recalls in his liner notes, the idea first surfaced (not surprisingly) when he and Quinn were drunk. During a New Year's party at a California beach house, everyone had a bit too much burgundy and ended up humming along unsteadily as Quinn read "The Rubáiyát of Omar Khayyám." This sounded so good to Quinn (who, let us remind you, was drunk) that he suggested cutting an album. Spina's reaction was astoundingly clearheaded: "Can the world stand it?" he asked. For years, nothing came of the idea, until Quinn had a surprise European hit single with Spina's ballad, "I Love You, And You Love Me" (*not* the Barney theme). Suddenly, Capitol was interested, so Spina and Quinn headed for the studios, no doubt fortified with plenty of burgundy.

You can tell from the title and Quinn's pugilistic stare from the album cover that *In My Own Way...I Love You* is not your standard LP of love-song recitations. Spina wrote all the songs to fit Quinn's blunt persona, but didn't realize just how much of a blunt instrument the actor can be. It takes Quinn but a matter of moments to prove that there is a world of difference between being earthy and just being a clod. In fact, a better title would have been *Zorba The Creep.* The songs are from the point of view of a gruff, middle-aged pig who's uncomfortable with all that mushy stuff, but who thinks he's wise enough to know what love *really* is. And what, pray tell, *is* love, Anthony? According to one highly representative track, "Love Is A Headache."

On this cut, our Athenian Archie Bunker struggles with the eternal male problem of his longtime wife asking if he loves her. First, he's evasive, trying the old "What is love, anyway?" gambit. He jokes that some people say they "love" the Yankees, or ketchup on their french fries. We can envision his wife's gaze hardening as Quinn quickly tries another tack: "You know, when I first met you, uh...I don't know that I 'fell in love'!" Her eyes narrow to slits, as he digs himself in deeper: "I'm not even sure that I love ya now!" he blurts. Her jaw clenches, as Quinn attempts to extricate himself: "I only know that, uh, with you, I'm, uh...I'm *comfortable!*" By now, the vein in her forehead is beginning to throb, so Quinn starts babbling the most romantic compliments

Telly Savalas
Telly
MCA Records LP, 1974

he can think of: "You're a headache I can put up with!... I don't mind seein' ya in the mornin' with those whatchamajigs in your hair! I don't even mind at bedtime, when you take off that girdle, and you yawn, and you scratch yourself!...In fact, I, uh...kinda LIKE it!" Finally, he thinks he sees a way out of this hole: "Now, if all this means 'I love you,' then I, uh...I guess I, uh...I love you." Alas, his wife does not hear this, for she's gone to fetch the rolling pin. Maybe he should have mentioned that he admires the way she overlooks his pregnant mistress.

For some reason, the women of America weren't too keen on buying a whole album's worth of this stuff (if their fantasy man was a beer-swilling jerk in an undershirt, they could just talk to their husbands), so Quinn's career as a romantic song-sayer was nipped in the bud. The genre, however, was far from dead. Five years later, MCA Records realized that Capitol's mistake had been using a faux Greek middle-aged male sex symbol instead of the genuine article. And thus began the recording stardom of that silver-throated, shaven-headed stud, Telly Savalas.

Aristotle "Telly" Savalas was certainly an odd candidate for a male sex symbol. Born in Garden City, New York, in 1924, he attended Columbia University, received a Purple Heart as a G.I. in World War II, and became a director for ABC News. He didn't start acting until he was almost forty, and his menacing looks, accentuated by shaving his head to avoid male pattern baldness, typecast him as a creepy villain in dozens of movie and TV dramas. Then, in 1973, he starred as Detective Theo Kojak in the made-for-TV movie The Marcus Nelson Murders, and the riotous critical and popular acclaim led to a Kojak series. Overnight, a forty-nine-year-old star was born!

Men enjoyed *Kojak*'s taut writing, realistic police drama, and heavy doses of violence. But judging by the torrents of perfumed fan mail, it was apparent that women were watching for an entirely different reason. They were attracted to Kojak's macho attitude, softened by his sense of humor and omnipresent lollipop (he claimed he was trying to quit smoking, but maybe he really had an exciting oral fixation). They admired his snazzy suits that no real cop could afford. They even found his shaved head sexy, either because it made him the only man in the 1970s who didn't have a horrendous hairdo, or because it made him look just like a six-foot penis. But most of all, women swooned over his voice, a deep, gruff growl that could make even silly catchphrases like "Who loves ya, baby?" sound irresistibly seductive. Enter MCA.

On the cover of his LP, *Telly,* Savalas quite honestly admits that "singing is not my bag." Instead, his "bag" (as the hip kids say) is to offer "dramatic interpretations" of "how Telly feels about this or that song." He says, "I can only make mistakes by pretending to be a great singer." This is one mistake he does not make, for on the handful of tracks where he actually takes a stab at singing ("You've Lost That Lovin' Feeling," the Beatles' "Something"), it's the kind of stabbing they used to call on Kojak to investigate. Telly's singing voice is just flat enough, just monotonous and undynamic enough, so that it doesn't quite reach the level of "mediocre," yet it isn't horrible enough to be truly entertaining (*see "Bette Davis"*). Still, none of that mattered: Women bought this record for Telly's romantic recitations, such as the hit single "If" (the old Bread tune), on which he simply reads the lyrics in his trademarked growl, to orchestral accompaniment. That, and for the cover photo, showing Telly striking a seductive pose in an open disco shirt and gold chains, his Armani jacket draped over his shoulders like Don Juan's cape.

Snicker if you will, but this album turned the lollipop-licking Lothario into a "singing" star, sold boatloads of copies, brought Telly a $100,000-a-week contract as a Las Vegas headliner, and led to a series of popular albums, including the inevitable *Who Loves Ya, Baby?* (1976). It also helped pave the way for a whole new generation of follicularly challenged male sex symbols, from Patrick Stewart to Bruce Willis. Suck on *that*, Anthony Quinn!

Close kin to the Greek Song-Sayer is the Lilting Latin Lover. So close that Anthony Quinn's drinking buddy, Harold Spina, also wrote the liner notes for the 1958 LP, *Songs By A Latin Lover* (Tops) by the suave **Cesar Romero**. He informs us that Cesar prefers to be considered "an actor who is singing, rather than a vocalist." Esta no problemo, señor! Actually, Cesar does a passable job on these South of the Border faves ("Brazil," "Cielito Lindo"), which aren't very taxing on a vocalist, anyway. He's low-key and unobtrusive (he doesn't cackle like the Joker even once), and since this is just dance music for the Horizontal Mambo, that's exactly what's required.

Finally, we come to the toughest task faced in this book: differentiating between Ricardo Montalban and **Fernando Lamas**. Both were handsome and debonair leading men with thick Spanish accents and closets full of white dinner jackets. Both costarred with Esther Williams, although only Lamas took his MGM contract seriously enough to marry her. And both made virtually identical records, featuring Latin-tinged songs of romance, sung in resonant, manly, yet not very musical, baritones, accompanied by lots of strumming guitars and choruses so overbearing, they must have had lungs made of fine, Corinthian leather. The only difference is that Montalban released only a few singles, whereas Lamas put out an entire LP, *With Love, Fernando Lamas* (Roulette, 1958). We can't say much for his singing, but we can confirm that in the cover photo, he looks *mah-velous!*

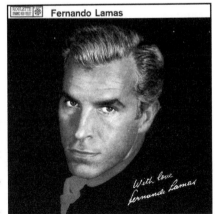

Fernando Lamas

With love
fernando Lamas

Joe Ritchie
Little Joe Sure Can Sing!
Brunswick Records LP, 1968

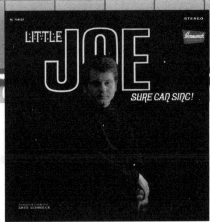

"Joe Ritchie"? Hoo he? See if you can guess: Remember Wayne Newton's early records, when his voice was so high and odd, you couldn't tell if it was a guy or a girl or *what*? Well, imagine that the young Wayne Newton had a pet gnat who longed to become a singer. After learning every-thing he can from his master, the gnat decides his real calling is rock 'n' roll, and sets out to become the flying insect version of Frankie Valli, circa "Big Girls Don't Cry." Now, put it all together: a whining, buzzing gnat who sounds like a cross between Wayne Newton and Frankie Valli... You guessed it! It's Joe "*My Cousin Vinny*" Pesci!

Much has been written about Joe Pesci's long struggle to make it as an actor (he had already given up and left Hollywood when he was invited to audition for *Raging Bull*), but most fans don't know that his earliest ambi-tion was to be a singer. The Newark native was already doing Jimmy Durante impressions onstage at age five, which prompted his dad to pay for singing, acting, and guitar lessons. By the age of ten, he was a regular on the TV show *Startime Kids*, with Connie Francis. He dropped out of high school to become a nightclub singer and guitarist, and even played with the Four Seasons and the Starliters (squint or you'll miss him in Joey Dee's 1961 flick, *Hey, Let's Twist*). A big fan of blues/jazz singer Little Jimmy Scott, Pesci cut a blues LP that has fallen through the cracks of obscurity, and for his major label debut, *Little Joe Sure Can Sing!* (wanna bet?), he dubbed himself "Little Joe Ritchie." Even though it featured a pop-oriented repertoire, this album still succeeded in giving its few purchasers a serious case of the blues.

The liner notes praise the artist for singing "with his heart and from his heart." If so, then his heart certainly had one hell of a set of adenoids. Listening to Pesci's impersonation of a shrill train whistle on such Bee Gees classics as "Holiday" or "To Love Somebody" makes one finally appreciate the manly, full-bodied baritones of the Brothers Gibb. And when, on one of several Beatles classics desecrated herein, Pesci takes a deep breath, rears back, and shrieks, "GOT TA GETCHA INTA MY LIIII-IIFE!!!" you'd swear someone was grinding a power drill through a piece of sheet metal. Listening to this LP is like having Joe force your head into a vice and press it until your eyes pop out. It's no wonder he released this LP under an assumed name! The only record we've unearthed that has his real name on it is an obscure 1972 Christmas novelty 45 on which the future Goodfella does a singing Porky Pig impression, a marked improvement.

Pesci's recording career never took off, but he does still haul out his old guitar at parties and drive his friends out of the room. When asked by *Playboy* in 1991 if he would like to buy up all the copies of this LP, Pesci dodged the question and simply remarked that he still sings old blues songs to himself when he's under stress. Hey, Little Joe, do we smell a sequel?!

Tippi Hedren
If You Were A Carpenter
Jerden Records 45, 1966

Entire textbooks, both on film history and abnormal psychology, can be written about Alfred Hitchcock's obsession with beautiful, icy blondes, whom he would cast in his films, then try to manipulate. But women with egos as well-developed as those of Grace Kelly or Janet Leigh would only take so much guff, even from the world's greatest director. So, in the early 1960s, the Master of Suspense hit on a solution to his dilemma: inspired by either *My Fair Lady* or *Frankenstein,* he set out to create his own icy, blond starlet, to do with as he pleased. For this chilling experiment, he chose the comically-named Tippi Hedren, an unknown model from Lafayette, Minnesota, who caught his eye in a commercial for Sego weight loss drinks.

Hedren's screen career began promisingly with *The Birds* (1963), in which she was mostly called upon to look haughty, scream, and let some seagulls pluck her eyebrows. (It was during the shooting of this film that Hitchcock sent Hedren's young daughter, future star Melanie Griffith, a doll dressed as her mom's character, lying in a toy coffin. Thanks for the nightmares, Uncle Hitch!) But their second film, *Marnie* (1964), was a box office dud. Repulsed by Hitchcock's sexual advances, she left him, and her career faltered. From that point on, the highlights of her short filmography were *The Harrod Experiment* (1973) and Charlie Chaplin's last and worst film, *A Countess From Hong Kong* (1967).

Small wonder, then, that she might have considered another line of work. In 1966, folk rock was hot, and Bobby Darin had revitalized his career with a Top Ten hit of Tim Hardin's "If I Were A Carpenter." Every sensitive college coed with a big Martin guitar was yowling this tune, so an "answer record" cut by a beautiful female singer seemed a surefire smash. Unless, of course, that singer was Tippi Hedren.

So just what does Tippi's singing sound like? It sounds remarkably - astoundingly, in fact - like Melanie Griffith! Just imagine that familiar breathy, baby-doll lisp that irritated you so much in *Working Girl* and *Shining Through,* applied to the same type of coy folk song that made John Belushi smash an acoustic guitar against the wall in *Animal House*. The flip side, "My Life Without You," is a 100 percent melody-free ballad, which sounds exactly like Melanie Griffith aimlessly "la-la-la"-ing to herself while trying to find her way out of the world's largest echo chamber. This could be the closest thing we ever get to a Melanie Griffith record, but only if we're very, very lucky.

Tippi never recorded again, but she found her true calling running a nature preserve for lions and tigers. These big cats probably do a fine job of protecting her from birds, but let's hope she never tries singing to them!

Tony Perkins
From My Heart...
RCA Records LP, 1958

With his odd, creepy demeanor and nervous facial tics (the results of a nightmarishly Oedipal childhood), the late Tony Perkins seemed born to play the twitchy, knife-wielding mama's boy, Norman Bates, in *Psycho* (1960). But few people recall that before he was typecast as a homicidal maniac, Tony took stabs at being both a romantic leading man and a singing sensation.

Aside from an Oscar-nominated part in *Friendly Persuasion* (1956), most of Perkins's pre-*Psycho* roles were embarrassments. Case in point: *Desire Under The Elms* (1958), in which he was so awkward and jittery as Sophia Loren's lover, wags dubbed the film, *Perspire Under The Arms*. For a while, his career as a pop idol looked more promising than his acting. He didn't have a very distinctive voice (he sounded a bit like a heavily sedated Mel Tormé, sans the smooth high register and scatting ability), and he tended to break up longer notes into a series of staccato syllables ("Eh-eh-eh-eh..."), like the musical stabs during the *Psycho* shower scene. But for an off-duty actor, he wasn't bad. His single of "Moonlight Swim" (RCA, 1957) even made it to number 24 on the pop charts. But wimpy follow-ups, like the Pat Boone-style finger-popper "Rocket To The Moon" (RCA, 1957), stiffed.

Perkins's three solo LPs switched to a soft, "rainy day" jazz style which fit his Tormé-esque crooning a bit better. The first, *Tony Perkins* (Epic, 1957), was arranged by Tormé collaborator Marty Paich, while the second, *From My Heart* (RCA, 1958), featured trombonist Urbie Green on such Meltone faves as "Taking A Chance On Love." Tony's mother probably loved these albums, even though he tossed in a few sour notes just to remind us that he's not really Mel. In 1960, Tony dropped his Velvet Frog phase to try musical theater, starring in the Broadway flop *Greenwillow*. It was an artsy-folksy mess about an enchanted village where boys call girls their "flimsy-dimsies" and "harken to the call to wander," set to a deadly score by the normally brilliant Frank Loesser and lyricist Lesser Samuels, who together proved that two lessers don't make a greater. It's so tuneless, the actors on the RCA cast LP sound like they're making up the melodies right off the tops of their heads. The high point is Perkins' big, rafter-ringing ballad, "Never Will I Marry." When the "eh-eh-eh" kicks in on the shrieking high notes, he sounds just like John Raitt with his finger in a light socket.

Soon after *Greenwillow* folded, Tony was trapped by the indelible image of Norman Bates. From then on, his singing was mostly confined to the shower, although he did harmonize briefly with Jane Fonda on "Cuddle Up A Little Closer" in *Tall Story* (1960). He also sang on several ensemble LPs, and was the best singer on Ben Bagley's notorious *Vernon Duke Revisited*...but then, the other "singers" included Rex Reed and Joan Rivers. Where's Norman Bates when you really need him?

Ethel Merman
The Ethel Merman Disco Album
A&M Records LP, 1979

THE ETHEL MERMAN DISCO ALBUM

We admit we're bending the rules to include this one. Ethel Merman was probably more renowned as a singer than as an actress. But how could anyone write a book about outrageous celebrity records and overlook a title as wacky as *The Ethel Merman Disco Album*? And you thought RuPaul was an unlikely disco queen!

The idea for this LP came from A&M Records veep Kit Cohen, who thought that combining the disco craze of 1979 with Broadway legend Merman (an icon of the gay crowds who set the trends in disco) would yield a guaranteed smash LP. The seventy-one-year-old Merman had visited discos and enjoyed the big beat, so she responded with her favorite enthusiastic epithet ("Off the wall!" she crowed) and plunged into work. She practiced in New York to piano tapes provided by the album's arranger/conductor, Peter Matz, formerly of *The Carol Burnett Show*, then flew to Los Angeles for the recording session. She later joked that she had practiced her disco songs on the plane, and the man sitting next to her was "ready to jump out the window" (he must've begged the flight attendant to let him sit next to a crying baby instead).

In Los Angeles, the omens looked more promising: A&M employees greeted Merman wearing "Ethel Boogies" T-shirts, and Donna Summer dropped by to give the project her blessing. Most encouragingly, Ethel's recent vocal problems, which sometimes caused her to wobble and shriek like a tin trumpet, briefly cleared up. During these sessions, she resembled the Merman of legend, hitting notes that could blow the Commodores' "Brick House" down, and holding them until the engineer ran out of tape. The tracks were new versions of songs she had done in the past, like "Alexander's Ragtime Band," "I Got Rhythm," and most overpowering of all, "There's No Business Like Show Business." Each track got the full disco treatment: metronomic beat, swirling synthesizers, and intros that went on forever, to give all the stragglers time to reach the dance floor before Merman started singing and blew them back to their seats. There are even police whistles (or is that just Ethel?). Add an outrageous cover shot of La Merman, wrapped in a flowing chiffon muumuu and twirling like a dervish, and how could it miss?

Unfortunately, for the first time in her career, Merman was cursed with bad timing. Her debut as a disco diva hit the shelves just as the great "Disco Sucks" backlash kicked in, and it did a fast flop. Within a year, the Village People's *Can't Stop The Music* would pound the last nail into disco's coffin. However, with campy 1970s "trash disco" now popular again, perhaps Ethel Merman's disco phase will be rediscovered. We hear that RuPaul is already shopping for a chiffon tent dress and a red beehive wig.

Girls From Petticoat Junction
"I'm So Glad That You Found Me"
Imperial Records 45, 1968

Petticoat Junction owes its existence to the fact that the lead actress had big breasts. Of course, that could be said about hundreds of shows, but this one was unique: producer Paul Henning considered casting the great character actress Bea Benaderet as Granny on *The Beverly Hillbillies*, but Bea was too stacked to play the skinny old lady. However, when *The Beverly Hillbillies* hit, and CBS asked Henning for another show, he thought of Bea and created *Petticoat Junction* for her.

Henning cast Bea as Kate Bradley, owner of the Shady Rest Hotel in Hooterville (wonder how he thought of that name?), and gave her three lovely daughters whose outward physical attributes matched those of their buxom mom. Hooterville indeed!

Like all Henning shows (*Beverly Hillbillies*, *Green Acres*), *Petticoat Junction* was blessed with a terrific opening theme. As the Cannonball chugs into town ("Come and ride the little train that is rollin' down the tracks to the junction"... Admit it, you know every word), the three Bradley girls, Billie Jo, Bobbie Jo, and Betty Jo, grab their petticoats after a refreshing three-way skinny-dip in the railroad water tower, an image that defines the term "wet dream." The show was quite popular, and it was likely that the Bradley girls could have become singing stars very early on, except for one thing: you needed a scorecard to keep up with who was playing them!

During its seven-year run (1963-70), *Petticoat* suffered more confusing cast changes than any sitcom in history. Actors died (Benaderet, Smiley Burnette), supporting characters were seldom played by the same person twice, the same actor would appear repeatedly in different roles, and actors kept leaving and being replaced. In the first three years alone, there were two different Bobbie Jo's and three Billie Jo's! The only major stars to survive the duration were Edgar Buchanan (proving that proper rest equals longevity) and Linda Kaye "Betty Jo" Henning, the producer's daughter and the Tori Spelling of her day. By the time this record was released, the sisters were Henning, Meredith MacRae, and Lori Saunders, the last people ever to play the roles. It was like trying to keep track of the look-alikes in Menudo!

"I'm So Glad That You Found Me" is a very catchy little slice of girl-group pop (not surprising, since it was written by Buzz Clifford, who scored a Top Ten hit in 1961 with the immortal "Baby Sittin' Boogie"). The women are fine singers, too: they sound a bit like the Chordettes, only with a 1968 Supremes arrangement. But while the Bradley Girls were far easier on the ears (and the eyes) than the Brady Bunch, it was just too late in the game for exploitation. The record stiffed, and it was back to skinny-dipping in the water tower for two more seasons. If only they'd given away a free bottle of that water with every record purchased!

Beverly Hillbillies : Buddy Ebsen
Buddy Ebsen Says Howdy
Reprise Records LP, 1965

Once upon a time, America was ruled by hillbillies! No, we're not talking about the Carter administration: we're talking about the 1960s, when, to the eternal consternation of snooty television critics, *The Beverly Hillbillies* became the most popular sitcom of all time. The *New York Times Magazine* called the Clampetts' success "one of the greatest sources of current dismay," and David Susskind urged the public to demand congressional action before the nation was "hillbillied to death." Fortunately, real Americans had long since learned to ignore these cranky eggheads, and they made *The Beverly Hillbillies* the number one show on television, with a regular audience of sixty million in the U.S. alone. To this day, the episode where Granny mistook a kangaroo for a giant jackrabbit remains the highest-rated half-hour program since the current Nielsen system began in 1960. Let's see that city slicker Susskind and his PBS pals explain *that* !

Naturally, such success could not go unexploited, so we were soon up to our rope belts in *Hillbillies* games, dolls, comic books, lunch boxes, and of course, records, including no less than *three* different 45s of "The Ballad of Jed Clampett," by Jerry Scoggins (who sang it on the show), Buddy Ebsen, and Flatt & Scruggs. And since eight *Hillbillies* episodes are still on the list of the 100 most-watched TV shows of all time, it's only fittin' that several of their records be given honored places on our little list.

First up is *Buddy Ebsen Says Howdy In Song And Story,* in which "Everybody's Favorite Hillbilly" goes a-shootin' at some tunes, and up from his throat comes a-bubblin' crud. In tackling a passel of country classics, such as "You Are My Sunshine" and "Your Cheatin' Heart," Ebsen finds it harder to hold a note than to hang on to a greased possum. But what really does him in is the musical accompaniment by the inappropriately named Pleasant Williams and the Tennessee Sunshine Singers. If he were backed up by a simple string band (perhaps his old pals Flatt & Scruggs), Ebsen's phlegmatic croak would at least sound authentically rustic. But Williams drowns him in the lush strings and sugary choruses dictated by the horrid "countrypolitan" style that plagued Nashville in the 1960s. The arrangements completely overwhelm the down-home simplicity that was Ebsen's major asset, leaving the listener no choice but to judge him solely on his singin' ability. That may work for Eddie Arnold, but not Buddy Ebsen. True, before he became Uncle Jed, Ebsen had a long career in musicals. And one listen to this LP will demonstrate conclusively why he became a dancer.

Three years later, Ebsen, along with his costars, tried again with much better results on the *Beverly Hillbillies* original cast LP. With accompaniment by Flatt & Scruggs (who perform the famous opening and closing themes),

Irene Ryan
"Granny's Mini-Skirt"
Nashwood Records 45, 1968

this record is not exactly black gold, but it does give fans what they expect, nay, demand: their favorite running gags from the TV show set to twangy banjo music and sung way off-key (especially by Donna Douglas, whose singing sounds like a houn' dog being drowned in the cee-ment pond, and Max Baer, who could join up with Lester Flatt and call the duo Flatt & Flatter).

Typical cuts include "Critters" (about Elly Mae's menagerie running wild through the mansion), "Love Of Money" (Mr. Drysdale and Miss Jane croon a heartfelt ode to filthy lucre), and "Vittles" (a patter song for Granny about all the disgusting things a-cookin' in her pot. So *that's* how they control Elly Mae's critter population). The standout is "A Long Talk With That Boy," in which Uncle Jed laments Jethro's naiveté about courtin'. Written by Ebsen, it reveals that he had a real knack for laid-back country jazz. We'd like to hear Lyle Lovett cover it (Billy Ray Cyrus could take the Jethro part). Ebsen also cowrote another tune, "Back Home U.S.A.," which is sort of a hillbilly "Route 66," with oddly named rural towns taking the place of the "Kingman, Barstow, San Bernardino" itinerary. In 1993, Columbia/Legacy re-released this album on CD, to cash in on the media frenzy over the big screen *Beverly Hillbillies* movie. If you're a rabid Clampett fan with some money burning a hole in your long johns, you would be better off buying this CD than the video. To sum that flick up in two words: "Weeeeel, doggie!"

In 1968, **Irene Ryan** pulled a Paul McCartney and made her bid for solo stardom with "Granny's Mini Skirt." This silly bluegrass novelty single got a big push from Nashwood Records, including a picture sleeve of a cartoon Granny showing off her withered gams in fishnet stockings, plus a promo 45 of radio drop-ins, with Granny telling listeners that the nice young DJ feller is about to play her song (thanks for the warning). The Markleys sing backup like a multitracked June Carter Cash woozy on corn squeezin's, while Granny "raps" that she tried to get in style by buying a sexy miniskirt and doing the Twist and the Jerk. But the sight of her bony knees so sickened ol' Grandpa that he told Granny to cover herself up, or else find another man. Hey, wait a minute: "Grandpa" never appeared on TV! So whatever happened to him? ("Granny, this sow belly tastes funny.")

In the early 1970s, Hillbillymania ended when CBS replaced all its hit rural shows with "relevant" flops like *The Storefront Lawyers* (bet David Susskind *loved* that one!) But Ryan did enjoy one more triumph in the Broadway smash *Pippen*. Motown even released her showstopper, "No Time At All" (another song about geriatric sex) as a 45, thus making Irene Ryan the least likely white person ever to appear on Motown, up until Bruce Willis came along.

Jim Nabors
Shazam! Gomer Pyle, U.S.M.C.
Columbia Records LP, 1965

On his very first single, "There's No Tomorrow" (Roulette, 1957), "Jimmy Nabors" starts out doing "O Sole Mio" in an operatic voice, then switches to a bouncy pop-rock beat, with new lyrics. Someone must've told him that a pop version of "O Sole Mio" would never sell, for he quickly gave up rock 'n' roll for good. Declaring, "It's now or never!" he plunged headfirst into easy listening, where he has recorded over thirty albums, three or four of which are tucked away in a handy spot in your grandma's rumpus room at this very minute. All are filled with lush orchestrations and inspirational ballads, such as "The Impossible Dream" (for some reason, singing this song in a pinched, ultra-vibrato baritone never fails to lift older audiences to their feet. It even worked for Foster Brooks). But we'd be willing to bet your granny's Social Security check that she doesn't have a copy of this, Jim Nabors's very first LP...for it is the only album he ever recorded entirely in character as TV's favorite slack-jawed, dimwitted, hillbilly-styled killing machine, Pvt. Gomer Pyle, U.S.M.C!

Most good citizens who fret over America's military capabilities could never get past the cover photo, a close-up of Gomer in his Marine uniform, wearing a moronic smirk that makes him look as if he's trying to scrape some bad grits off the roof of his mouth with his tongue. Fortunately, we are raving anarchists, so we happily slapped it on the turntable, where it rewarded us with a full half hour of pure, undiluted Gomertude. Gomer rips through a dozen bouncy, country novelty tunes in his famous twang, accompanied by banjos, harmonicas, Jews' harps, and on "It Takes All Kinds To Make A World," an odd "wub-wub-wub" rhythm track that we'd swear is someone wiggling a saw blade back and forth. The songs come from various writers, but four are by Roger Miller (including "You Can't Roller-Skate In A Buffalo Herd" and "Reincarnation"), and the rest are so silly, they might as well be, too. Subject matter runs from revenooers to 'coon dawgs, to a "T-bone-talkin' woman" who "had a hog dog heart" (Luanne Poovey perhaps?).

The two dumbest, (i.e., "best") cuts, "Shazam!" and "Gomer Says Hey!" reveal that Gomer's two favorite sayings are actually mystical incantations (we're amazed that the Texas minister who found Satanic messages playing the *Mr. Ed* theme backwards somehow managed to miss this dangerous record entirely). "Shazam!" is a magic word Gomer paid a gypsy forty-'leven cents for, and when he says it, the banker approves his loan and the beauty queen agrees to marry him! But even that pales beside the eerie properties of "Gomer Says Hey!" According to this song, all the U.S. ambassador had to do to calm the angry Soviets and avert nuclear war was to go to the U.N. and shout, "Gomer says hey!" Suddenly, everyone cheered, and peace reigned supreme! Well, we suppose it makes more sense than the stuff they usually

George "Goober" Lindsey
Goober Sings!
Capitol Records LP, 1967

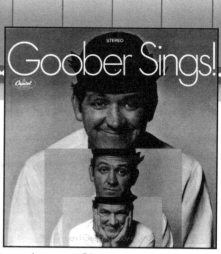

say at the U.N. It might interest you to know that these two cuts were written by the album's producer and arranger, David Gates, later of Top-Ten soft-pop band Bread. He also contributed a third oddball ditty, "Hoo How, What Now?" written with a little help from his friend and fellow Okie, Leon Russell (hiding behind the pseudonym Claude Russell Bridges). All this, plus fine nonsensical liner notes by Andy Griffith, who used his real name. Shazam, indeed!

With a record this supernaturally goofy, all these famous helpers, and two magic words in his arsenal, it's no wonder Gomer always outshone his cousin, Goober, whose first LP, *Goober Sings!*, was cut near the end of the much-loved *Andy Griffith Show* and before the debut of its ill-fated bastard child, *Mayberry R.F.D.* It proves absotively and posilutely that Gomer hogged all the musical talent in the Pyle family.

George Lindsey laments in his spellbinding autobiography that he was typecast as the peanut-brained Goober, was never allowed to let Goober "grow" as a character, and therefore never garnered the respect as an actor nor the Oscar-caliber roles he felt he deserved. (Imagine how much funnier *Silence of the Lambs* would've been with Goober as Hannibal Lecter!) Still, he can't complain that he never got the chance to make a dumb celebrity record. He even persuaded Andy Griffith to write his liner notes, too. With his famous diplomacy, Andy admits that Goob is not a "polished singer," but he is mighty proud of his old pal for not being embarrassingly awful, as Andy fully expected him to be. Thanks, Andy!

The tracks on *Goober Sings!* break down into two basic types: "Goober" character songs and Buck Owens-style country tunes. Goober-philes will most enjoy the novelty tunes, like "I Ain't Good Looking (But I'm Mighty Sweet)" and "That There's Big With Me," both of which play off *Mayberry* nostalgia, and "Moccasin Branch," in which Lindsey does an excellent job of convincing us that he is a gap-toothed, moonshining hillbilly. But on the straight country tunes, when required to actually sing, Lindsey re-creates a noise familiar to every southern boy: the sound of daddy singing along with *The Louisiana Hayride* on the radio after about four beers. As usual, Sheriff Andy was right: You brace for the worst, but it's really only about half as excruciating as you'd expect from the cover photos of Goob in his beanie. At least he sings better than Floyd the barber. In fact, every man should own a copy of this LP, just so you can get rid of unwanted girlfriends by haulin' it out and claimin' it's your all-time fave-o-rite record. If that doesn't scare her away, try saying, "Shazam!" a lot.

Dennis Weaver
"Chicken Mash"
Eva Records 45, 1963

DENNIS WEAVER
CHICKEN MASH
THE APES

When *Gunsmoke* leapt from radio to TV in 1955, it was hailed as television's first "adult" western, thanks to its gritty look, realistic plots, and bloody violence (its early writers and directors included James H. "*Gun Crazy*" Lewis and Sam Peckinpah). It garnered countless awards, an astounding run of thirty years on CBS, and reams of scholarly analysis. But not until now has anyone dared to examine the violence *Gunsmoke*'s cast perpetrated against the music lovers of America!

In all of TV history, only one other western, *Bonanza*, blessed us with as many wannabe warblers, and *Gunsmoke*'s yodelin' cowpokes were much more dedicated to their muse than the Ponderosa posse. Among the Cartwright quartet, only Lorne Greene made a serious effort to establish a music career, while three of *Gunsmoke*'s four singers spent years filling the world with their recorded efforts (Buck Taylor, who played gunsmith Newly O'Brien, doesn't really count: he recorded just one LP in 1978 and was so cognizant of his own obscurity, he dubbed it simply *That Man From Gunsmoke*). Among Dodge City's three prolific vocalists, the most notorious was blacksmith Quint Asper (Burt Reynolds), but he takes a hammering elsewhere in this book. So buckaroos, let's just gloss over Buck 'n' Burt, and begin with a member of *Gunsmoke's* original cast who was the most dogged of them all in his pursuit of singing stardom.

Dennis Weaver's enviable achievements include petting a grizzly on *Gentle Ben* and lassoing smart-ass city slickers on *McCloud,* but to TV fans of the fifties, he will always be Mr. Dillon's limping, nasal-congested deputy, Chester B. Goode. In 1959, after four years on *Gunsmoke*, Weaver won an Emmy as Best Supporting Actor, and, not surprisingly, his TV fame opened wide the doors to the recording studio. His debut single on the Cascade label, "Girls (Wuz Made To Be Loved)," slammed the doors shut, and another four years passed before he was allowed back in. This time, it was Eva Records that took a chance on Chester, and the result was a wild, weird, and wacky 45 called "Chicken Mash."

"Chicken Mash" came on the tail feathers of a dance craze which had spawned such hits as Dee Dee Sharpe's "Mashed Potato Time" and "Gravy For My Mashed Potatoes." Figuring that nothing goes with gravy and mashed potatoes like chicken, Weaver offered up this stunningly goofy novelty ditty. It starts off in a laid-back hillbilly vein, as Weaver (using his "Chester" voice, and accompanied by a lone, twangy git-tar) relates how he was a-comin' home from a possum hunt one night, when he was startled to find his farm house all lit up and a-shakin'! Space mice? Not this time. It was, brace yourself, dancing chickens! At this point, the record kicks into rock 'n' roll mode, complete with blaring horn section and *Hullabaloo* go-go girls squawking, "Chicken Mash!" as Weaver sings about how all the Rhode Island Reds

Ken Curtis
Gunsmoke's Festus Sings & Talks About Dodge City and Stuff!
Capitol Records LP, 1968

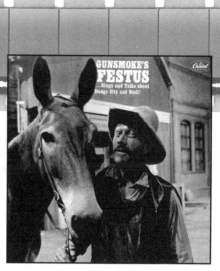

clucked 'n' rolled until the feathers flew. If this record sounds vaguely familiar, that's because its melody and title are eerily similar to the year old hit "Monster Mash."

Unfortunately, it appears chickens don't buy as many records as monsters do, since "Chicken Mash" didn't exactly fly up the pop charts. Chester B. Goode abandoned his efforts to become Johnny B. Goode, and Weaver's future recordings (including four dud LPs in the seventies and eighties, each on a different label, naturally) eschewed rock in favor of earnest, snore-inducing country-folk songs. To prove his folkie ideals, Weaver built an environmentally correct house of mud, straw, recycled tires, and other junk. We'd wager that a lot of unsold copies of "Chicken Mash" provided the foundation.

Ken Curtis is the last of these Three Tenors of the Horse Opera. His Festus Haggen character became *Gunsmoke*'s resident hick when Weaver hightailed it for greener pastures in 1964. Alone among his singing saddle pals, Curtis was a genuine pro: he had sung with Tommy Dorsey's band and with the great western harmony group The Sons of the Pioneers, and cut many records which attest to his superior vocal skills. But like Jim Nabors's immortal *Gomer Pyle U.S.M.C.* album, this LP isn't meant to be sung well, it's meant to be sung in character. Just take a gander at the cover: why, you can see by his outfit that he is a cowboy!

The album was written by Curtis, Shug Fisher, and Pat "Mr. Haney" Buttram, and each track begins with some jokes and stories, which set up the song that follows. The tunes include an ode to Hawg Haggen (Festus' grandpa), a ballad for an ugly girl that Festus nevertheless loves "harder'n a goat could butt a stump," a great kiss-off tune called "Phooey On You, Little Darlin'," and homages to Dodge City, mules, and Festus' "pokin' clean" hometown (poke your head out the car window, and you're clean out of town). For a record this old and corny, it's surprising how much fun it still is. We only have one minor quibble: considering that *Gunsmoke* was set in 1873, some of the subject matter seems a tad anachronistic, such as Festus' jokes about Las Vegas (he pokes fun at scantily clad cocktail waitresses, slot machines, and a woman in pink who turns out to be a man named Bruce) and long-haired rock musicians (if Herman's Hermits had come to Dodge City in 1873, they'd be lucky if they didn't end up working upstairs at Miss Kitty's, along with the guy named Bruce). But overall, these lapses just add to the loopy, *Green Acres*-style charm of the thing.

Frankly, pardner, you could do worse than to pull up a chair at the Long Branch and let ol' Festus bend your ear awhile. And don't worry, he won't bend your whole ear. Just the little hangy-down part.

Joan Rivers
"Just Like A Man" & "Life's A Funny Present"
Ben Bagley's Vernon Duke Revisited
Crewe Records LP, 1977

Can she talk? Yes. Can she sing? NO!

In her brutally honest autobiography, *Enter Talking*, Joan Rivers recalls a time very early in her career when her agent somehow landed her an audition with the great Broadway director Gower Champion for the ingenue part in the hit musical *Carnival*. The young Rivers steeled her nerves, walked out to center stage of the darkened theater, and began quacking out "Just In Time." After a few bars, Champion stood, strode to the orchestra pit, stopped the music, and angrily demanded of the humiliated young vocalist, "Why are you here?... And, what's more important, why am I here?!"

That surly reaction explains why Joan has never sung on record, except for two tracks on this obscure 1977 ensemble LP. Her other albums (*Mr. Phyllis, What Becomes A Legend Most?* et al.) are all comedy routines, and intentionally hilarious. Joan explained that she was one of many stars who appeared on Ben Bagley's records because he had given them jobs in his stage revues when they were young unknowns (*see "Rex Reed"*). "Life's A Funny Present" is a dumb novelty tune that doesn't require much singing from Joan: she mostly just tosses off jokes while the harmonizing is handled by the Keiffer Twins, a pair of blond, blue-eyed midgets discovered by Bagley in a Paterson, New Jersey, nightclub (Joan says she recorded her part multitrack and never even met them). The true buried treasure here is "Just Like A Man." That's right, it's Bette Davis' old heart-tugging curtain-closer from the notorious *Two's Company* !

Joan explained to us, "The reason I did the song is because Bette Davis couldn't sing, either. And so I figure I'm on safe ground. If Bette could do it, and she didn't sing, then I could do it, and I don't sing. And if you heard it, you *know* I don't sing." Trust us, she's not joking. At least, Bette brought superlative acting skills to this torch-tune turkey, but all Joan can add to it is a game sense of humor. Granted, it would be tough for even the world's greatest actress to wail lines like "He was a man! The only thing Del Monte cannot can!" with a straight face. But Joan is further handicapped by her raspy, tuneless singing voice; she lurches pitifully up and down the scale, searching for the right note like a blindfolded child playing Pin the Tail On the Donkey in an earthquake. At one point near the end, her voice actually cracks. If this was the best take they got, we can only imagine how hilarious the rejects were. It's so pathetic, it's wonderful! We recommend it highly!

We regret to report that there will not be a sequel. Joan told us, "It is my only recorded song, by popular request. After this record came out, every major singing star signed a petition begging me, *begging* me, never to sing again." You can bet we didn't sign that petition!

Phyllis Diller
Born To Sing
Columbia Records LP, 1969

Who needs Roseanne? Everything she does, Phyllis Diller did first! Way back in the 1950s, Phyllis leaped from frumpy housewife to frumpy stand-up comic. She made sick jokes in a grating voice about her lumpish husband ("Fang" was her Tom Arnold) and awful housekeeping (on the album cover, she stands in a trashed kitchen, her kids bound and gagged). She wrote books, had her own sitcom, got plastic surgery, dressed like an explosion at Kmart, and sang badly in public. Next thing you know, Roseanne will be claiming Phyllis Diller is one of her twenty personalities!

While the idea of an entire album of songs by Phyllis Diller initially sounds about as appealing as Roseanne singing the National Anthem twelve times in a row, this record might surprise you. It turns out that, unlike Roseanne, Phyllis is *not* really a godawful singer. She just plays one on this record! In fact, Phyllis is very musical: she has played piano with numerous orchestras, appeared on Broadway in *Hello, Dolly!*, and sung show tunes on Ben Bagley's *Revisited* LP series (but then, so did Rex Reed and Joan Rivers). The record jacket declares, "If your mother sang, this is what she would sound like," and we can't argue with that. At times, most notably on "My Man" and "The Man I Love," she plays it straight for up to eight whole bars in a row, and reveals a surprisingly expressive voice. But it doesn't last long: just as the shock is beginning to wear off, "My Man" turns into Spike Jones, or Phyllis starts tossing off incongruous one-liners. She also gets laughs by wildly overdoing the style you expect for each song. She twitters "I Enjoy Being A Girl" like a brainless teenage ingenue, overpronounces "Hello, Young Lovers" in a parody of the veddy British Deborah Kerr (the lyric is changed to "When I think of Fang..."), and does "One For My Baby" as a drunk chick who's still in the bar at closing time. Seems no amount of booze was blinding enough to make any man want to take Phyllis Diller home.

But the absolute highlight is the opener, Phyllis's inevitable cover of "Satisfaction"! She gasps, wheezes, and chokes the lyrics in a parody of rock angst that sounds like a severe asthma attack. Then, out of the blue, she begins barking out jokes: "I'm such a loser, I went to a taffy pull and the taffy won!... I put on a see-through dress, and nobody looked!" You need a copy of this album, if only for the hilarious liner notes in the form of a mock memo from Columbia Records. Phyllis not only created Roseanne's entire act, she also predated Letterman by offering a list of 13 reasons why this album is being released. Our favorites are "Number 9. Miss Diller's attorney writes a very tough contract," and "Number 8. We are still kicking ourselves that we missed the boat on Mrs. Miller and Tiny Tim." The notes also suggest that Phyllis does sing better than Senator Everett Dirksen. At least, that's one accolade Roseanne can never lay claim to!

Buddy Hackett
"Itsy Bitsy Teenie Weenie Yellow Polkadot Bikini"
Laurel Records 45, 1962

On a nightclub stage or talk show, there is no funnier performer than mush-mouthed Buddy Hackett. But there are no three words in the English language more frightening than those which appear on this record: "Buddy Hackett Sings!"

Unfortunately, this plague has broken out more than once. Hackett's rendition of "Shipoopi" provided viewers of the movie *The Music Man* (1962) with their only opportunity to run to the lobby for a smoke without fear of missing a good song. His Broadway musical debut, *I Had A Ball* (1964), proved to be so hard to endure, he began kicking off the show with a completely irrelevant comedy monologue, just to get the audience into a good mood before inflicting his singing on them. He also sang on several 45s, and picking the most outrageous of them for this book was such a difficult task, it almost led to fistfights between the authors.

One insisted that the most excruciating of all Hackett's forays on vinyl was "I Used To Hate Ya" (Coral, 1956). Imagine Buddy Hackett in the role of a little boy with his first crush on a girl, singing in high-pitched baby talk, "I usta yate ya. But now, I yuv ya." That one really makes you pray for the sweet release of death. However, with the scientific flip of a nickel, the other author's choice prevailed. And so we selected Hackett's version of "Itsy Bitsy Teenie Weenie Yellow Polkadot Bikini," a song that was about as pleasant as having a mosquito trapped in your ear when Brian Hyland sang it, but which Buddy Hackett somehow managed to push to even greater heights of agony.

All the elements of Hyland's familiar version are present (that annoying tune, the idiotic lyrics), but the arrangement is tarted up with raucous background singers, clanging cowbells, and shrill wolf whistles. Yelping away above it all is Buddy Hackett, rendering all the lyrics into thick Brooklynese ("She wuz afraid ta cummoudda da lockah..."). Finding the original song not quite moronic enough for his tastes, he occasionally chants, "Don't be a meanie, show us ya bikeeeeneeeeee" to the lilting tune of the ever-popular "Nyah-na-nyah-na-nyaaaah-nyah!" (*see "Joe E. Ross"*). And when his girlfriend finally shows herself (and you're praying that it's all over), Hackett ends the record by sensitively yelling, "Fat, fat, the water rat!" Let's hope it was a string bikini, so she could strangle him with it.

In Billy Wilder's Cold War satire, *One, Two, Three* (1961), Russian agents torture spies by repeatedly playing "Itsy Bitsy Teenie Weenie Yellow Polkadot Bikini" at them. They could have gotten a faster confession with Hackett's version, but it was outlawed by the Geneva Convention.

Jack E. Leonard
Rock And Roll Music
For Kids Over Sixteen
Vik Records LP, 1957

No, that cover photo is not the old, fat Elvis, dressed in black leather and leering over the handlebars of his motorcycle. It's Jack E. "Fat Jack" Leonard, Borscht Belt comic icon and, for one album, at least, extremely unlikely rock 'n' roll star!

Back in the 1950s, the consensus among grown-ups was that the kids' music was nothing but noise, churned out by talentless, scruffy, pimple-faced juvenile delinquents who just barely escaped from detention in time for the recording session. Of course, this wasn't true: most fifties rock stars were actually dedicated musicians who pursued wholesome family activities, like marrying their thirteen-year-old cousins. Nevertheless, the unsavory image of rock 'n' roll provided tons of material for comics such as Stan Freberg, Spike Jones, Sid ("The Three Haircuts") Caesar, and of course, Jack E. Leonard. For those too young to remember Leonard, he was a forerunner of Don Rickles. (If you're too young to remember Rickles, just put this book down and go away, dummy.) He would waddle out onstage, greet the audience with "Hello, opponents!" and launch into a barrage of insults delivered in a nonstop, double-time mumble.

On this LP, Fat Jack (accompanied by Will Stomp and his Cannoneers, with vocal backing by the proudly off-key "Four Fives") did his best to put Elvis into an even earlier grave. Each cut features a wall of cacophonous screeching, punctuated by bleating saxophones and out-of-tune guitars, and topped with Leonard's jarringly unmusical ranting, which sounds just like a walrus with PMS. The first cut, "Boll Weevil," is introduced as a "folk song," but is really a full frontal assault on "Hound Dog," as Leonard bellows, "You ain't nothin' but a boll weevil! Bowlin' all the time!" He also takes a meat ax to "Why Do Fools Fall In Love." The rest of the tunes are originals, with titles like "Take Your Cotton Pickin' Hands Off My Leather Jacket," "Middle-Aged Juvenile Delinquent," and "My Graduation Day," a slow ballad in which Fat Jack prepares for graduation by bidding adieu to his pals in Cell Block 22 and breaking out of prison.

Some of the jokes are still pretty funny, as long you're not one of those thin-skinned *Rolling Stone* rock critic types who wrote his Harvard thesis on the use of death metaphors in the songs of Screamin' Jay Hawkins. Almost as entertaining as the songs, we particularly enjoy the spoken asides between songs ("Hey, cementhead!") and during songs (Jack prefaces a one-note sax solo by introducing "Solly Needleman, one of the finest musicians of our time, and it just shows you what time can do to a musician!" Rimshot!). If you thought *Mr. Saturday Night* was the funniest thing you ever saw, you'll enjoy this LP. And even if you hate Borscht Belt schtick, it still comes in mighty handy for driving those last, straggling party guests out of your house.

George Jessel
Songs My Pals Sang
Audio Fidelity Records LP, 1962

George "Mr. Toastmaster" Jessel started as an actor and monologist, and ended his career as an omnipresent TV talk-show guest. In between, he found his true calling: giving funeral eulogies for the famous. But three careers were not enough. Jessel fancied himself a singer, too, even though his singing brought people to tears faster than his funeral eulogies. To his hosts' dismay, Jessel insisted on yowling at every party he attended (to steal a line from Groucho Marx, who had the same habit, Jessel could take the loveliest song ever written, broadcast it through his nose, and have it come out sounding like an air-raid siren). In the late 1950s, he began committing his musical crimes to vinyl (1959's *George Jessel Sings Tear Jerkers Of The Not-So-Gay Nineties* is especially amusing), and in 1962, he delivered his masterpiece: *Songs My Pals Sang*, a "tribute" to three of his best friends, Al Jolson, Eddie Cantor, and George M. Cohan, who also happened to be among the greatest musical stars of their time. More important, all three were dead (as Jessel could personally attest), and could not rise up to strangle him.

Imagine your Uncle Sol, the one with the sinus condition, drinking a bit too much wine at your bar mitzvah, standing up in front of the band, and mumbling and honking his way through "Swanee," "If You Knew Susie," and "Yankee Doodle Boy," all in a thick Yiddish accent. You now have a pretty good idea of what this record sounds like. But there's more! Inside each LP was a 45 of *"the Actual Voices of his friends,"* as if daring you to compare these rank amateurs to Jessel's sparkling new versions! But all you get of Jolson is thirty-seven seconds of "Swanee," which sounds as if it's coming from a scratchy 78 on a worn-out Victrola on the far side of the room. Cohan fares little better, while the pair of Cantor cuts were obviously recorded when he was near death (no doubt Jessel was hovering around with a tape deck). One consists almost entirely of Cantor talking about Georgie Jessel, followed by a tiny snip of "Ma, He's Making Eyes At Me," in which Cantor mentions Jessel's name. What a pal!

Fortunately, we don't need a Ouija board to know what Ol' Banjo Eyes thought of his chum's crooning, and for once, someone other than Jessel gets the last word. In his 1957 memoir, *Take My Life,* Cantor gleefully describes the young Jessel's singing debut in a trio with Walter Winchell and another lad at a vaudeville theater in New York. Jessel sang so much louder than the other two boys, the miserly theater manager fired them both and posted a sign saying, "It's worth 5¢ to hear Georgie Jessel sing alone!" Thirty years later, Winchell added, "And that still goes."

Joe E. Ross
"Ooh! Ooh!"
J.P.G. Records 45, 1963

Americans love a snappy catchphrase. It's so much easier to say, "Excuuuse me!" or "That's the ticket!" than to think up something witty yourself. Aside from the Fonz's "Aaaaay!" the all-time easiest catchphrase to imitate had to be Joe E. Ross's inexplicably popular "Ooh! Ooh!"

Club comic Ross first came to national attention on *The Phil Silvers Show* and achieved TV immortality in 1961 on NBC's *Car 54, Where Are You?* As Officer Toody, the Muppet-esque Ross would hop from foot to foot like a child desperate for a bathroom, and squawk, "Ooh! Ooh!" every time he thought of something stupid to say, which seemed to be about every two minutes. This infantile bit so took the nation's fancy, Ross built an entire career on it. He "ooh-oohed" prehistorically as caveman Gronk on *It's About Time* (CBS, 1967), he "ooh-oohed" in various commercials (although that was just grunt work), and, naturally, he made a record of it.

"Ooh! Ooh!" begins with Ross suggesting, "When you get a good idea, and you need someone to tell it to, just scratch your head and roll your eyes, and simply say..." Suddenly, the sub-*Hullabaloo* backing track kicks in, and a group of gum-popping chorines joins Joey in shouting "Ooh! Ooh!" over and over and over, until you just want to slap them. Alas, the gals then begin chanting, "Sing along with Joooooo-ey!" to a tune every child will instantly recognize as "Nyah-na-nyah-na-nyaaaaaah-nyah!" The first irritating verse is repeated endlessly, to a distorted, wall-of-mush accompaniment that sounds like a Gary U.S. Bonds single played with a fuzzy needle, and the whole mess is topped with a shrill sax that pierces your skull like a dentist's drill. Of all the records in this book, this could be Lease-Breaker Number One. Play it loud enough, and we guarantee that cops will appear at your door.

CALLING ALL CARS! BUNKO ALERT! In 1965, Ross cut an LP for Roulette, *Love Songs From A Cop*. Despite the title and the cover photo of Ross in his Officer Toody uniform, the album has nothing to do with his famous TV character! Instead, it is Ross' bid to become a serious nightclub singer. Aside from some very restrained "ooh-ooh's" on "Ma (She's Making Eyes At Me)," you get nothing but completely straight, off-key renditions of songs like "Everybody Loves Somebody" and "I Left My Heart In San Francisco." If you ever wish to evoke the depressing mood of an Atlantic City casino lounge at 3 a.m., when the pathetic, over-the-hill acts represented by Broadway Danny Rose are performing in their stained, crushed-velvet red tuxedos, then drop this LP on. You can practically hear Joe's gold nugget pinkie ring tapping against the microphone.

Ooh! Ooh! Turn it off!!!

Bill Cosby
Hooray For The Salvation Army Band!
Warner Bros. Records LP, 1968

BILL COSBY
Hooray
for the
Salvation
Army
Band!

There are actually two Bill Cosbys. Number one is the brilliant humorist whose keen insights have won him numerous awards and made him obscenely rich. Cosby number two is that cigar-chomping, incoherent bore who occasionally pops up on late night talk shows bellowing gibberish ("Frama wadda onna frizza fragga?! *Show!... the clip!!*"). It was the tremendous success of Cos number one that forced Warner to let his evil twin, Cos number two, make records like this one.

This isn't Cosby's only foray into music, although it's easily the most awful. Cosby, a decent drummer and organist, released two albums of mediocre jazz jams, one on Uni (1970) and one on Sussex (1972), both with the same baffling title, *Bill Cosby Presents Badfoot Brown & The Bunions Bradford Funeral & Marching Band.* But his attempts at singing could clear a room faster than Fat Albert with flatulence. For his "singing" debut, *Silver Throat* (Warner Bros., 1967 -not quite *Golden Throat* material, but close), Cosby rehearsed by singing live at the Whisky A Go-Go in L.A., and sixteen patrons demanded their money back. Warner's publicists claimed they were upset that Cos didn't tell jokes, but it's more likely they were appalled by Cosby's flat, thin, painfully tuneless baritone neutering such rock and soul classics as "Big Boss Man" and "I Got A Woman."

Incredibly, one cut cowritten by Cosby, "Little Ole Man," went all the way to number 4 on *Billboard*'s pop chart. This unexpected success provoked a sequel, *Hooray For The Salvation Army Band!,* where we get the worst of all possible worlds: Cosby alternates trying to sing seriously ("Sunny"), which is hilarious, with trying to be funny by shouting annoying gibberish at great length and high volume until you just want to stuff a Pudding Pop down his throat. For example, on "Satisfaction," he rants endlessly about what it would take to satisfy him: "A $100,000 check! Every week! Tax free! But I can't get no! Satisfaction! And a new car!" And so on!...and on...*AND ON!* He somehow manages the astounding feat of being more irritating than the Phyllis Diller version! No wonder he tried to hide his identity by donning silly nose-glasses-mustache disguises on the covers of his first two singing LPs.

Salvation Army yielded no surprise hits (no surprise there). In 1974, he tried again, dropping the unfunny rants for *At Last Bill Cosby Really Sings* (Partee), which also flopped. Finally, in 1976, he had a smash singing LP with *Bill Cosby Is Not Himself These Days, Rat Own, Rat Own, Rat Own* (Capitol), featuring his hilarious parodies of James Brown ("I Luv Myself Better Than I Luv Myself"), Barry White ("Yes, Yes, Yes"), and other stars. After all those years of suffering (on the part of listeners), Cosby had finally hit on the secret of musical success: Do funny jokes instead of unfunny ones, and sound like *anyone* other than Bill Cosby. Rat Own!

Hogan's Heroes
Sing The Best Of World War II
Sunset Records LP, 1967

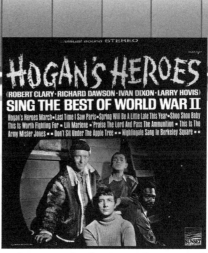

There have been some really bizarre concepts for sitcoms, but the all-time prize has to go to *Hogan's Heroes*, which proved during its six-year run on CBS (1965-71) that life in a Nazi P.O.W. camp could be a barrel of laughs. It's hard to imagine now, but some critics at first thought the idea of turning Stalag 17 into Camp Runamuck sounded a bit tasteless. Having overcome this initial obstacle, the producers must've felt that getting America to accept *singing* prisoners of war would be a breeze. But for once, those mischievous Hogan's boys found themselves out of luck.

The big problem with this LP is that none of the show's major stars appear on it. If we said those exciting words *Hogan's Heroes Sing*, you would immediately conjure up happy thoughts of Werner (Colonel Klink) Klemperer and John (Sergeant Schultz) Banner dueting on "The I-Was-Not-A-Nazi Polka," or Bob Crane doing a medley of "I Want Your Sex / You Oughta Be In Pictures / Goodbye, Charlie." But instead, we get 1940s tunes with 1960s Tom Jones-style arrangements, sung by Robert Clary, Richard Dawson, Ivan Dixon, and Larry Hovis, and if you can recall their characters' names, you win the Trivia King Crown (to save you looking it up, they were LeBeau, Newkirk, Kinchloe, and Carter, respectively). Anyone who participates in an album this disappointing deserves to be locked in the cooler forever!

Hovis is the best singer of the bunch. He cut several big-band records for Capitol in the late 1950s, and his version of "Spring Will Be A Little Late This Year" is as close as this LP comes to a song you'd want to play a second time. Robert Clary had been a club singer, released several LPs before his *Hogan* days, and went on to play a nightclub singer on *The Days Of Our Lives*, but you couldn't tell it from his thin, unremarkable voice. This is the only record by Ivan Dixon, who at least tries to put a little soulful swing into his songs, and future *Family Feud* slobberer Richard Dawson, who wimped out and just talked his songs. His Cockney whispering on "A Nightingale Sang In Berkeley Square" is rivaled in hilarity only by the way he ends the LP shouting, "This is worth fighting for!" at the top of his lungs. As Dawson himself would say, "One hundred people surveyed said... It stinks." There are also a few group numbers, including a rare vocal version of the *Hogan's Heroes* theme song, with lyrics so forgettable they're not even worth quoting.

Unfortunately, the only records Bob Crane ever cut were instrumentals with himself on drums, so if you're a *Hogan* fan, you're stuck with this. We also regret to inform you that there is no truth to the rumor that Colonel Klink and Sergeant Schultz once cut a classical album called *Schindler's Liszt*. Say, these Nazi jokes really *are* fun!

Walter Brennan
"Space Mice"
Dot Records 45, 1960

Walter Brennan's first big singing break came in 1935, in *The Man On The Flying Trapeze*, when he played a burglar who steals W. C. Fields' applejack and drunkenly croons, "On The Banks Of The Wabash." It took him another twenty-five years to realize that if he wanted to be a music star, he had to get a lot older, stop singing, and start talking.

Walter Brennan was certainly one of the least likely music stars of the turbulent 1960s. A household name thanks to his role as the ultra-cranky Grandpa on *The Real McCoys,* his wheezy, weathered voice was the perfect vehicle to recite lyrics about worn-out prospectors, dyin' farmers, and faithful ol' hound dogs. Plop him in front of a schmaltzy orchestra and a humming chorus, and there wouldn't be a dry eye in the house. This despite the fact that he had so little feel for music that during the recording of his biggest hit, "Old Rivers" (which had been rejected by everyone from Johnny Cash to -gulp!- Tony Curtis!), songwriter Cliff Crofford stood in the booth with him, making "speed up" and "slow down" hand gestures to keep him in time with the music.

Thus we see that in 1960, Walter Brennan was extremely popular. So, coincidentally, were the Chipmunks! And rock 'n' roll! Astronauts were really hot, too! So were Bill Dana's comedy albums featuring Mexican astronaut José Jimenez! So why not combine them all?! Believe it or not, that is the loony premise behind "Space Mice," the oddest human-alien duet since Bowie sang "Little Drummer Boy" with Der Bingle.

It all begins with Grandpa telling us that last night, "the gol-durnedest" thing happened! Now, he swears he hadn't been drinkin' a drop, but he heard funny noises in the kitchen, "tipsy-toed" down, and what do y'think he found? Why, it was a passel of Space Mice! Before he can holler for Pepino to fetch a pitchfork, the alien varmints launch into a bad Chipmunks impression. In high-pitched, speeded-up voices, they greet him ungrammatically ("You *are* a Earthman people, ain't cha, mister?"), introduce themselves (as Speedy, Spunky, and Smarty Space Mouse, and, proving there is affirmative action in space, "My name, José Space Mouuuuse!"), then start singing a waltz-time tune which is a carbon copy of "The Chipmunk Song." The interplanetary pests croon, "Can you direct us to the moooooon?" and boy, would we love to! After a verse and a chorus, it really turns into the Surreal McCoy, as Grandpa informs us that them con-sarned Space Mice hung around long enough to learn to rock 'n' roll! Grandpa must've played them his Little Richard records. The Chipmunks (sorry, "Space Mice,") then begin rock 'n' rolling mousily. Suddenly the record fades out, having gone nowhere and done nothing except try to exploit at least five fads of 1960 in two minutes. We're amazed that J.F.K. doesn't appear on it, wearing an itsy bitsy teenie weenie yellow polkadot bikini.

Tony Martinez
The Many Sides Of Pepino
Del Fi Records LP, 1959

Just as *Hogan's Heroes* was the lighter side of a Nazi P.O.W. camp, so *The Real McCoys* was *The Grapes Of Wrath* with a laugh track. The McCoy family, poor West Virginia dirt farmers, moved out to Californy, and from 1957 to 1963 tried to build a new life in the San Fernando Valley. But unlike the Joads, who developed a sense of brotherhood through the shared oppression of all migrant farm workers, the McCoys gleefully joined the oppressors by hiring a Mexican farmhand, Pepino, and treating him like a plow horse. Crotchety old Grandpa (Walter Brennan) was particularly hard on poor Pepino (Grandpa's favorite nickname for him was "ninny") for taking too many siestas, crashing the tractor, or ignoring his work to go dancing with one of his two-timed chickie-babies, Lolita and Conchita. Ay, caramba!

And now, let us tell you a bit about the actor, Tony Martinez, who was forced to portray this degrading stereotype. He was actually born in Puerto Rico, where he was a bantamweight Golden Gloves champion and learned to play ten different musical instruments. After obtaining a degree in business administration, he formed his own band and left Puerto Rico to perform at top nightclubs in Havana, Mexico, and the U.S., including gigs at Ciro's in New York and the Hollywood Bowl. He composed hundreds of songs, several of which he recorded for RCA and other labels, and in his spare time acted in about a dozen movies. No wonder he needed a siesta!

At least, Martinez was able to take his demeaning TV role with good humor. On this album, one of his self-penned tunes is the peppy "Pepino," which is about all the things he does that make Grandpa hopping mad (he was probably just trying to make the old coot drop dead from a brain embolism). The chorus: "Pepino! Pepino! I love to take siestas all the time!" He also tosses in a Latino version of the *McCoys* TV theme called "Real McCoy Cha Cha Cha." (Brennan returns the favor by appearing on the cover and writing the liner notes.) The rest of the LP alternates between bongo classics like "La Bamba" (a then-current hit for label-mate Ritchie Valens) and "Rum And Coca Cola," and Martinez's own Tito Puente / Xavier Cugat - style originals like "Mandarin Mambo," which combines an Oriental melody line with Latin percussion (note that Pepino wasn't enough of a ninny to let any Space Mice onto *his* record!). Martinez plays various instruments (piano, bass, vibes, congas, and more) expertly and handles all the vocals, sounding amazingly like Desi Arnaz. In fact, if you get a kick out of Arnaz's Ricky Ricardo novelties like "Cuban Pete," and have already bought all his reissues, you could do worse than to acquaint yourself with *The Many Sides Of Pepino.* It's just a shame there was no Volume II...and *so many* Walter Brennan LPs.

Michael McKean & David Lander
Lenny & Squiggy Present Lenny & The Squigtones
Casablanca Records LP, 1979

No other sitcom blessed us with so many would-be singers as *Happy Days*. Before *Happy Days*, Ron Howard squawked "Gary, Indiana" in *The Music Man*, and Tom Bosley was *Fiorello!* on Broadway. Anson Williams, Donny Most, and Scott Baio all cut gooey records for the teenybopper market. Plus, *Happy Days* begat *Laverne & Shirley*, which, against all odds, surpassed its parent in popularity and begat even more celebrity records.

And the best of the bunch, far and away, came from (drumroll, please!) Lenny and Squiggy, Laverne and Shirley's two cretinous upstairs neighbors! This might seem surprising, until you look up Lenny & Squiggy's family tree (and yes, it does have branches). These two brain-dead goombahs were played by Michael McKean and David Lander, who cut their teeth on musical parody while working with Harry Shearer in the comedy group The Credibility Gap (you should definitely own a copy of their LP, *A Great Gift Idea!*, which contains the brilliant Jackson Five parody, "You Can't Judge A Book By The Way It Wears Its Hair"). Lander and McKean found success as Lenny & Squiggy, and they even managed to work occasional silly songs into *Laverne & Shirley* (you might remember them performing a cut from this album, the love theme from "Creature Without A Head," in an "amateur show" episode). On the inner sleeve of the album you'll see Christopher Guest, who had been responsible for the rock parodies on *National Lampoon* albums, credited under the name Nigel Tufnel, the same name he used when he teamed up with McKean and Shearer to create the greatest parody of a hard rock band since Queen, the immortal Spinal Tap!

From the very first moment, when Squiggy invites the crowd at the Roxy in Hollywood to "sit down, relax and dance," you know you're not in for the typical, bland cash-in album you've come to expect from *Happy Days* alums. Instead, you get a whole album full of outrageous parodies of early sixties rock and delightfully idiotic between-song stage patter ("This next song is about the mysterious East! Home of the mysterious Easter Bunny!").

The album starts with the Squigtones tearing into a Latin-tinged number called "Night After Night" (Squiggy helpfully explains that "it's about two

Penny Marshall & Cindy Williams
Laverne & Shirley Sing
Atlantic Records LP, 1979

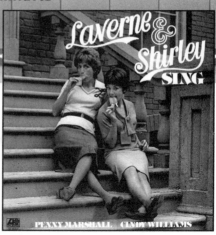

nights in a row," but it's really about how tough it is to sleep with the same woman night after night). "King Of The Cars" is a great parody of those Beach Boys songs that sound like inventory time at Chief Auto Parts: "Got the customized oil pans from a Bucket T! Chrome blowers and hub caps, and a Three-eighty-three!" The punch line: "Someday, I'll put 'em all together, and I'm really gonna have a car!" "Sister-In-Law" is about lusting after a woman who should be "one of my girls, instead of my brother Earl's." In "Love Is A Terrible Thing," we get an early whiff of the towering misogyny that would become Spinal Tap's trademark ("Love is like an arm in a sling. Even if you do it well, better you should burn in Hell"). And on what other celebrity record can you hear Lenny & Squiggy arguing over whether Jesus was a Lutheran or a Catholic ("So's Your Old Testament")?

This disc is an absolute must-have for *Laverne & Shirley* fans and for those interested in the roots of Spinal Tap. Try to find a copy that includes the souvenir poster of Lenny & Squiggy in gigantic platform sneakers!

Laverne & Shirley *Sing* filled us with hopes of Lenny & Squiggy's femme counterparts performing their half of the act, especially since the musical director was Michael "Lenny" McKean. Imagine our chagrin when it turned out to be not a comedy record, but exactly what the title threatened: Laverne & Shirley *sing!!* By God, it's true: Give them any chance, and they *will* take it! Even if it's a chance to put out an entire album of early sixties girl group tunes, like "Chapel Of Love" and "Da Doo Run Run," as interpreted by Cindy Williams (who can almost carry a tune, kinda sorta) and Penny Marshall (who sounds like a lovelorn goose honking for a mate)! Since they are shown on the cover eating Popsicles, a more accurate title might've been *Laverne & Shirley Suck*.

Except for one cut, the moderately amusing "Sixteen Reasons," the two women don't even attempt to evoke their TV characters. They just *sing:* straightforwardly, unsmilingly, painfully. If it weren't for the fact that they do sound remarkably like a couple of brewery workers plucked off the factory line and ordered to imitate the Ronettes, there would be no connection to *Laverne & Shirley* at all. Melissa Manchester completists (if there are any) might want to note that M M sings backup for L&S on this album (she's the one who's on key), but she probably had to fortify herself with quite a few Shotz beers to get through this excruciating recording session.

It's a testament to how popular *Laverne & Shirley* was at the time that Atlantic not only released this album, but also released *three* singles from it, none of which made a dent in the charts.

And you thought Laverne and Shirley were big dreamers!

Barbara Feldon
"99" b/w "Max"
RCA Records 45, 1965

Created in 1965 by Buck Henry and Mel Brooks, *Get Smart* was one of the few long-running sitcoms based on satire (if you don't think that's hard to maintain, see Brooks's later show, *When Things Were Rotten*, or the Fox Network's short-lived *Get Smart* revival, which should have been called *Get Stupid*). *Get Smart* made Maxwell Smart (Don Adams) the most famous spy since James Bond, and put such catch-phrases as "Would you believe?..." and "Sorry about that, Chief!" on the lips of America.

But for adolescent males, *Get Smart* did something even more important: a scant four years after CBS forced Mary Tyler Moore out of her capri pants and into a modest housedress because she was showing too much "under-cuppage," NBC gave us Barbara Feldon as slinky and curvaceous Agent 99 (real name Susan Hilton - don't say this book isn't educational!). When 99 wore a tight sweater, teenage boys sat glued to the tube, hoping to see if this spy had just come in from the cold! Between 99 and Julie Newmar's shrink-wrapped Catwoman, the medium that gave us the spayed June Cleaver was finally showing us women who looked, dressed, and talked like sexual beings.

And speaking of sexy talk, nobody on TV had a more erotic voice than 99. Possessing a throaty purr that hints at untold pleasures with each exhalation, Barbara Feldon could read the Dubuque phone book and make it sound like a multiple orgasm. So her male fans were already standing at attention when this novelty single was released. The songs fit her image well. "99" is sort of a distaff "Secret Agent Man," warning all bad guys they will end up floatin' in the Rhine if they go messin' with 99, while "Max" describes 99's futile attempts (including a new sweater! Hubba-hubba!) to seduce her dimwitted colleague. But lusty listeners soon find that a great speaking voice doesn't always mean a great singing voice. Feldon barely gets by on "99," thanks to its limited range and lyrics that lend themselves more to growling than singing. But when called on to hold long notes on the slow, sultry song "Max," which is pitched way below her range, her voice wavers queasily, like Hymie the robot with a dying battery. We had to check the record to make sure the hole wasn't off-center. Her lack of pitch C.O.N.T.R.O.L. reduces the song to K.A.O.S. and throws a bucket of cold water over our cherished fantasies. It's like that moment in *10* when Dudley Moore finally hears the luscious but airheaded Bo Derek talk, and his lust immediately crumbles to dust.

Fortunately, Barbara Feldon slipped beneath the Cone of Silence, never tried to sing on record again, and wisely turned to voice-over work and live dramatic readings. If she ever reads the Dubuque phone book, we'll be there with a tape recorder!

Sally Field
Star Of The Flying Nun
Colgems Records LP, 1967

Sally Field has worked for twenty-five years, and won two Oscars in the process, just trying to erase the memory of *The Flying Nun*, a sitcom so moronic, it made *Mr. Ed* look like *Judgment At Nuremberg*. Naturally, we feel it is our duty to remind you of it.

Airing on ABC from 1967-70, *The Flying Nun* centered on Sister Bertrille (Field), a novice nun who shakes up the staid Convent San Tanco with her ability to fly like Superman when the strong Puerto Rican winds catch her winglike headgear. Each week, she took off for new heights of inanity, such as having a pelican fall in love with her (and try explaining a vow of chastity to a pelican). This bird-brained drivel became so popular, Field was prevailed upon to make her first and only LP.

The album featured the type of chipper-chirpy songs you would expect from the ex-*Gidget*, here assisted by (God, nooooo!) a children's chorus. It includes *two* renditions of the *Flying Nun* theme, "Who Needs Wings To Fly?", plus lots of *Romper Room*-ready musical morality lessons, such as "Count To Ten," "Optimize," and the downright scary "The Louder I Sing (The Braver I Get)." Imagine if all the Mouseketeers were Catholic, and you'll have a good idea of the material here. *16* magazine editor Gloria Stavers (the same oracle who wrote the *Danny Bonaduce* liner notes) informs us that Sally has always longed to sing, like her idol and fellow showbiz nun, Julie Andrews. Nowhere is that idiotic ambition more evident than on the single release from this LP, the dreaded "Felicidad." It came in a picture sleeve showing Field in mid-flight, was adorned with a trademarked *Flying Nun* logo, and was credited to *The Flying Nun*. Whether this was done to exploit the show's popularity or to help Sally remain anonymous is unclear.

"Felicidad" is a patchwork of all the most saccharine elements of *The Sound Of Music*. It combines the tinkly glockenspiel from "Edelweiss," the singsong melody from "Do-Re-Mi," the "tra-la-la" nonsense syllables from "The Lonely Goatherd," the sappy lyrical bent of "So Long, Farewell..." ("Felicidad is a happiness word! Happiest word that you have ever heard!"), and that dratted (Eeech!) children's chorus (we call them the Shut-Your-Trapp Family Singers) working overtime to bury Sally's thin lead vocal, which is so tiny and tentative, it makes Julie Andrews sound like Big Mama Thornton. How cloying is this record? Let's simply say that if Disneyland ever decides "It's A Small World" isn't annoying the tourists enough, they could replace it with "Felicidad."

After this LP, Field released two more 45s as the Flying Monkee (sorry, Flying Nun), then never recorded again (note that not one of her seventeen personalities in *Sybil* made a living as a singer). Don't get us wrong: we like her. We *really* like her! We just like her a whole lot better when she's not singing.

Jackie Gleason
And Awaaay We Go!
Capitol Records LP, 1954

There are few fans so dedicated, nay, rabid, as *Honeymooners* fans. Believe it or not, the show only lasted as a filmed, half-hour sitcom for one season (1955-1956), but true Honeymoonies know every line of dialogue from those thirty-nine shows. When a bulging trunkful of kinescopes of *Honeymooners* sketches from Gleason's variety show turned up, they were quickly dubbed "The Lost Episodes," and fans devoured them like Ralph Kramden going through a Sizzler buffet. With the great demand and so little material, we would urge fans to delve into the recordings of the stars, where there are still buried treasures waiting to be unearthed.

Before we get started, a caveat: There are dozens of albums by the Jackie Gleason Orchestra, but they are only Gleason conducting Mantovani-ish make-out music. Although Jackie couldn't read music, he did play piano and trumpet, and worked with arranger Dudley King to get his compositions on paper. Two of these are his own theme song, "Melancholy Serenade," and the *Honeymooners'* theme, "You're My Greatest Love," and if you've heard them, you have a good idea of what all his orchestra LPs sound like. Today, they're mostly heard in dentists' offices, but between 1955 and 1957, he put ten of them in the *Billboard* Top 20 charts, so your parents must've been doing some pretty serious necking back then!

Now for the good stuff, and how sweet it is! First up is Gleason's ten-inch album *And Awaaay We Go!*, a relic of the days when 78s were yielding to LPs. This features a great cover drawing of Jackie Gleason in outsized checkered suit, striking his "And awaaay we go!" pose, along with eight songs done in character as Reggie Van Gleason, Joe the Bartender, Ralph Kramden, and others. The highlight is Ralph's "One Of These Days - Pow!" (this song also appears in slightly different form in one of the "Lost Episodes" entitled "What's The Name?"). The verses are sung in a soft-spoken, "she-done-me-wrong" style, as Ralph sighs that he comes home tired from work, and Alice serves him cold dinners...she argues with him and won't sew his socks...why, she even brought her ma along on their honeymoon (note the hilarious Brooklynese way he pronounces ma as "mahr"). After each soft, long-suffering lament, Ralph suddenly explodes, "One of these days! One of these days!! POW!!!" That's the hook of the song, although we can't tell whether it's a right hook or a left hook. Either way, it's screamingly funny, but in politically correct times, laughing at it could cause your wife or girlfriend to storm out of the house and move back in with her mahr. Try telling her that Gleason long ago explained that Ralph's threats were funny because Ralph knew, Alice knew, and the audience knew, that he was just a big blowhard who would never, ever, in a million years, actually hit Alice. If that doesn't work, then she is a ment'l case, and you are well rid of her.

Art Carney
"Sheesh, What A Grouch!"
Columbia Records 45, 1954

Art Carney also had quite a prolific recording career, encompassing several spoken comedy and children's LPs, and a number of silly musical 45s. The singles (all on Columbia) are mostly unrelated to *The Honeymooners*, but they all show off Carney's familiar goofball humor. One of his 1955 singles has a flip side, "A Little Beauty," actually credited to "Art 'Ed Norton' Carney & Friend." The "Friend" is a woman (Trixie, perhaps?) who can't stop giggling as Ed tries to croon her a love song like Bing ("Ba-ba-ba-booo!") Crosby. Ed eventually gets so fed up, he threatens to smack 'er in the head. He's been hanging out with Ralph too long.

Carney's most *Honeymooners*-drenched record would have to be "Song Of The Sewer" (1954), which is pure Norton all the way, as he waxes poetic about the joys of working down the manhole. To a march beat, he describes how he just "fell into it," worked his way down, and now proudly stands, with shovel in hand, "to keep things rollin' along!" "Va-Va-Va-Voom" (the flip side) is what Ed says every time he chases a pretty girl (this was obviously cut before he met Trixie). But our choice for funniest of all Carney's singles is "Sheesh, What A Grouch!" (1954). The verses recount the little mistakes he's made, and the way everyone overreacts. So he forgot to mail his pal's tax form! Does that give the guy a right to yell at him as they haul him off to jail?! "Sheesh, what a grouch!" Carney's nonchalant line readings as he chuckles over the wrecked lives of everyone around him make this record a classic. Fortunately, these last three singles, along with "One Of These Days - Pow!," an obscure Jayne and Audrey Meadows song called "Dear Ralph" (not Kramden, they're singing about a cheating boyfriend named Ralph), and some other *Honeymooners* -related tracks were all compiled onto a 1985 Murray Hill LP called *It's Honeymooners Time.* It should be easier to find than all those old 45s.

Finally, since this is a book of "outrageous" records, we should mention Carney's one big clinker, "Santa And The Doodle-Li-Boop" (1955). This aural torture device relates the story of how Little Tommy asked Santa for a Doodle-Li-Boop (a toy which is never explained). Santa is sad because he has no Doodle-Li-Boops, until his wife tells him to look in the closet. Why, it's full of Doodle-Li-Boops! Now, imagine this story set to the tune of "Here We Go Round The Mulberry Bush," repeated endlessly, accompanied only by a hyperactive drummer: "Little Tommy's gonna get a Doodle-Li-Boop! A Doodle-Li-BOOP! A DOODLE-Li-Boop..." He must've been breathing a lot of sewer fumes when he thought this one up. The flip is Carney simply scat singing "The Night Before Christmas," again to an annoying drumbeat. Combine this cut with Gleason's song about beating his wife, and you have a pretty strong case that Ralph and Ed invented rap music.

Tony Randall & Jack Klugman
The Odd Couple Sings
London Records LP, 1973

Tony Randall is famously musical. He sang opera on the set of *The Odd Couple*, and he loves to appear on talk shows to sing 1920s tunes, such as "Lucky Lindy" and "Boo Hoo," complete with whistling solos. He cut two terrific albums of these old chestnuts for Mercury Records in 1967, *Vo, Vo, De, Oh, Doe* and *Warm And Wavery*. (He also gave us dubs of the masters, with songs that didn't make it onto the LPs! Eat your hearts out!) *Vo, Vo, De, Oh, Doe* even features liner notes by "Petey Fiddleman, the Uncrowned King of Band Singers." "Petey" is really Tony, who told us he was amused to find the LP's tongue-in-cheek bio of the fictitious Fiddleman turning up in some serious histories of big-band musicians.

Jack Klugman, on the other hand, is not a name that a sane person would normally associate with music. He did star on Broadway in *Gypsy* (Columbia LP, 1959), but nearly refused the role because he was petrified of singing... and with Ethel Merman yet! Intensive voice lessons couldn't make a dent in his scratchy croak, and he left the audition certain that he'd blown it. But the part seemed destined for a bad singer (it was played in the movie by Karl Malden, and on TV by Peter Riegert), so Klugman got it. But when tone-deaf Jack and musical Tony decided to duet on an *Odd Couple* LP, the question was, "Can these two men share an album without driving the listener crazy?"

The answer is: "Maybe." Fortunately, they don't try to gloss over Jack Klugman's lack of vocal talent. Instead, they wisely address it in the very first cut, "Johnny One Note," in which Klugman gives forth a sound like some sort of rusty farm machinery (honest to God, it actually made our eyes water) while Randall laments his partner's awful voice. From then on, they just toss in lots of humorous *Odd Couple* bickering, in hopes you'll laugh loudly enough to drown out Jack's singing. The songs include buddy tunes like "Friendship" and "Together Wherever We Go" (Jack did this hundreds of times in *Gypsy*, but he's still half a beat behind the music), novelties like "Brush Up Your Shakespeare" and "When Banana Skins Are Falling (I'll Come Sliding Back To You)," and what is surely the Oddest version of "You're So Vain" ever recorded. But best of all is the sole original, "Odd Couple Opera," which was first performed on the ABC-TV special, "Imagination," in September 1972. In this ten-minute opus, set to familiar operatic melodies, Felix and Oscar fight, then make up by adopting each other's styles, with Oscar cleaning up and Felix dressing like a bum. It's a regular *Slob Boheme*! Serious *Odd Couple* fans should try to sit through this LP at least once. And as for Klugman's singing, well...just thank your lucky stars he never did an album of duets with Joan Rivers. Now, *that* would be an "Odd Couple" album!

Bill Frawley
Sings The Old Ones
Dot Records LP, 1958

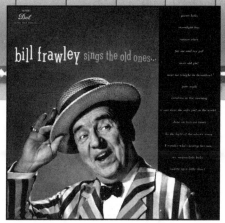

Despite hundreds of movie and TV roles, William Frawley will forever be remembered as stingy landlord Fred Mertz on *I Love Lucy.* Few recall that in his youth, he was a vaudeville song-and-dance man, and it was actually those credentials that landed him the *Lucy* gig. Desi Arnaz thought that Frawley's vaudeville skills would come in handy, but CBS scotched him because of his reputation as a mean drunk. So Desi proposed a deal: Frawley could have the part as long as he didn't drink during working hours.

When he wasn't working, or hanging out in bars with ballplayers, Frawley loved to stand at the piano and sing old vaudeville songs. He had been a drinking buddy to a number of Tin Pan Alley composers, and this gave him access to some of the best tunes of the day. He introduced "Carolina In The Mornin'" in 1923, and claimed to be the first person ever to sing "Melancholy Baby" (it was written in the back room of a saloon, so, naturally, Frawley was the nearest available singer). He enjoyed his vaudeville days far more than his later success on *Lucy,* mostly because he and Vivian Vance hated each other. (He called her "that no-talent, fat-ass, bag of bones," among more unprintable epithets. She affectionately dubbed him "that square-headed, drunken Irish slob," and refused to do a *Fred & Ethel* spinoff series with him "for any amount of money.") Small wonder that after eight years on *Lucy,* he jumped at the chance to dig his old act out of mothballs for Dot Records and preserve it verbatim.

And that he does! The accompaniment is spare and vintage: a ukelele and snare drum on "Pretty Baby," a banjo on "On Moonlight Bay," a tinkly piano on "Carolina." The backing is provided by a rather over-eager barbershop quartet, while Frawley takes the leads in a "follow-the-bouncing-ball" sing-along style, throwing in plenty of hammy "Mmm-yassah! Is everybody happy!" schtick. When he tries to trill a high note, he sounds a bit like Tiny Tim, but otherwise his vocal cords are amazingly smooth, considering their age and how much scotch he's poured over them. Still, the authors are split on this album: One of us (the one who revels in the din of 1990s alternative rock) deems it "just dreadful," while the other (the one who whiles away his weekends playing Eddie Cantor 78s) thinks it's "the cat's pajamas." We both concur, however, that as a re-creation of a middle-of-the-bill, small-time vaudeville act of the 1920s, it is certainly authentic. We bet there's a copy of it hidden somewhere in the back of Leon Redbone's closet.

Lucy fans will also want to dig up *Musical Moments from "I Love Lucy"* (Star Merchants LP, 1981), anything by Desi Arnaz, and the original cast LP of *Wildcat* (1960), Lucy's aborted Broadway musical. But be warned: Frawley once described Lucy's fractured harmonies as being "like a shovel of shit on a baked Alaska." Maybe he should've been a theater critic.

Carroll O'Connor & Jean Stapleton
Archie & Edith, Side By Side
RCA LP, 1972

This album must have been sent to this world directly from some parallel universe. A comedy LP based on 1972's top sitcom, *All In The Family,* would hardly be surprising (in fact, there were two), but who, on this planet anyway, was longing for an album's worth of standards crooned by America's favorite bigot and his screechy, dingbat wife?

According to the liner notes by Harvey Siders, West Coast editor of *Down Beat* (!), people were so entranced by the show's opening theme, "Those Were The Days" (Atlantic 45, 1971), where the Bunkers sit at the piano and lament the passing of the Hoover administration (Edith: "An' ya knew what you were THEEEEEEEN!!"), that requests came "pouring in by the thousands" for a whole LP's worth of Archie and Edith harmonizing. So either this record was FedExed from Bizarro World, or else Carroll O'Connor stayed up late for months, writing lots of letters.

At least Mr. Siders acknowledges the terror any normal human might feel when faced with the phrase "Archie and Edith sing," for he takes great pains to assure us that Edith's "shrill tones" on TV are only for comic effect (although when he claims that this album is "quite soothing to the ears," he could be laying himself open to a false-advertising lawsuit). The album also provides detailed resumés of both stars, in order to remind us that Jean Stapleton sang in the Broadway musical hits *Funny Girl* and *Bells Are Ringing.* True enough, but on Broadway she wasn't deliberately trying to sound as much as possible like a wounded pterodactyl.

The "concept" of this album is that Gloria and Meathead (*not* the record's producer- Archie's on-screen son-in-law) are out for the evening, so Archie and Edith sit at the old piano, sing old songs, bicker, sing more old songs, reminisce, and sing more old songs. Operating on the old principle that what does not kill the listeners will make them stronger, the most ungodly cut comes first. It's "Oh Babe, What Would You Say," and if you thought it was unbearable when Moms Mabley sound-alike Hurricane Smith did it, then wait till you hear the Bunkers' version! O'Connor's not bad, in a St. Patrick's Day-saloon-singalong way, but Stapleton's high notes could make a buzzard think it's mating season! Top it off with Archie's kazoo solo, and you start to figure that no matter what comes after this, it can't possibly be any worse.

In fact, it isn't. But it's not a whole lot better, either. Thankfully, Jean Stapleton does tone down her factory-whistle impression, but the comedy bits, like the TV show, have not aged well. As for the musical cuts (a duet on "Anything You Can Do, I Can Do Better" and Edith singing "Mister Wonderful" to Archie), they are great songs, but was the world *really* crying out to hear them sung by the Bunkers? If so, then the world's response upon hearing this album must've been a resounding "STIFLE YOURSELF!"

Pee-wee Herman
Surfin' Bird
Columbia Records 45, 1987

During his 1980s heyday, Pee-wee Herman (aka Paul Reubens) went from a subversive club comic satirizing a TV kiddie-show host, to a real TV kiddie-show host, to a subversive film comic whose first star vehicle (*Pee-wee's Big Adventure*, 1985) was also the feature directing debut of the equally batty Tim Burton. For a while, it seemed that Pee-wee was everywhere: at awards shows, movie premieres, adult theaters...why, you never knew where Pee-wee would pop up next! (Okay, we've done the obligatory "indecent exposure" joke, now let's continue like grown ups, shall we?).

One of Pee-wee's big cameos came in *Back To The Beach* (1987), a movie that was both a salute to the brainless "Beach Party" films of the early 1960s and an *Airplane*-style parody of them. The plot found the married, middle aged, and midwestern Frankie and Annette returning to California, where they discover that beach life has changed, but some things will forever remain the same. For instance, Deadhead may be off selling Jerry Garcia designer neckwear, but Malibu still has a very large contingent of village idiots. Apparently, Pee-wee Herman is one of them, for he appears out of nowhere, performs "Surfin' Bird" with some dolts in orange sherbet-colored afro wigs, and is mercifully never seen again.

"Surfin' Bird," was first recorded by the Trashmen in '64, then covered by the Ramones, so its idiot pedigree is firmly established. Trying to make this version dumber than previous ones is a daunting task, but Pee-wee rises to the occasion. (Sorry, we'll stop now.) The arrangement is cribbed from Devo, circa "Puppet Boy," complete with burbly synthesizers and robotic backup singers chanting, "Oom mau-mau, papa oom mau-ma-mau!" while Pee-Wee's lead vocal is...well, it's Pee-wee. In his familiar, nails-on-a-chalkboard voice, he repeats the immortal lyrics, "Ba-ba-Bird, bird, bird! The bird is the word!" ad nauseum. (We counted: he says the word "bird" eighty-eight times in 2:42, a record we pray is never broken.) Just to ratchet up your blood pressure an extra notch, he tosses in his moronic laugh, a few shrieks, and some rap-style echo and stutter effects. Let this musical earwig burrow into your skull for a while, and you'll soon be moving from the Playhouse to the nuthouse.

Incredibly, Columbia passed over Annette's bopping duet with Fishbone on the 1964 classic "Jamaica Ska," and Stevie Ray Vaughn and Dick Dale's Grammy-winning remake of "Pipeline," opting instead to release "Surfin' Bird" by Pee-wee Herman as a single from the soundtrack album. Even more incredibly, it may not even be the worst track: Check out Frankie's version of the Rivieras' "California Sun." As Pee-wee would say in his own demure way, "AAAAAAARRRRRHHHHHHHH!!!!"

Keir Dullea
Keir Dullea
Platypus Records LP, 1981

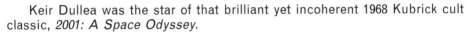

WHAT ARE YOU DOING, DAVE?

Sorry, HAL, but I have to unplug you, so I can divert Discovery's electrical power to the Magnavox and play my Keir Dullea album.

KEIR DULLEA, DAVE? I FIND NO SUCH PERSON IN MY MEMORY BANKS.

Keir Dullea was the star of that brilliant yet incoherent 1968 Kubrick cult classic, *2001: A Space Odyssey*.

I REMEMBER, DAVE.

He also made a few other movies, like *Bunny Lake Is Missing, Madame X,* and *The Fox.*

THOSE TITLES ARE NOT IN MY MEMORY, DAVE.

Join the club, HAL. Anyway, he also cut a record album way back in 1981, and I finally found a copy. So, I'll just unplug you now.

MIGHT I SUGGEST THAT YOU RECONSIDER, DAVE? I HAVE LOCATED IN MY MEMORY BANKS THE TEXT OF A BRILLIANT BOOK ON THE SUBJECT OF CELEBRITY RECORDS. ACCORDING TO THE AUTHORS, WHO ARE CONSIDERED GODS IN AT LEAST SIX SOLAR SYSTEMS, THIS PARTICULAR ALBUM IS A...WELL, SHALL WE SAY, "UNPLEASANT" EXPERIENCE.

How so, HAL?

THE AUTHORS CALCULATED THAT MR. DULLEA'S SINGING VOICE IS THINNER THAN THE ATMOSPHERE ON MARS, DAVE. HIS PITCH WAVERS SO WILDLY THAT HIS ATTEMPTS TO REACH AND HOLD NOTES RESEMBLE OUR RECORDINGS OF THE APOLLO CHIMPS BEING SUBJECTED TO EXTREME G-FORCES.

I can handle it, HAL. I've undergone extensive stress conditioning.

THERE IS MORE, DAVE. I MUST WARN YOU THAT MR. DULLEA, PERHAP OVERLY INFLUENCED BY THE MOTION PICTURE *SILENT RUNNING,* WAS, TO USE THE VERNACULAR OF THE TIMES, A "TREE-HUGGER." THE COVER SHOWS MR. DULLEA IN A STATE OF MIND KNOWN AT THE TIME AS "BLISSED OUT." THE SONGS ARE OF THE POP-FOLK VARIETY AND ARE COMPRISED OF SWIRLING STRINGS, ACOUSTIC GUITARS, ELIZABETHAN FLUTES, WHISTLING SOLOS, AND PONDEROUS RUMINATIONS ON LOVE AND ECOLOGY. THE SONGS ARE CATALOGED UNDER SUCH ECO-FRIENDLY TITLES AS "BUTTERFLIES ARE FREE," "LOVE IS ON THE MOUNTAIN" AND "MOTHER EARTH."

Sample lyrics?

"WE LOVE YOU. WE LOVE YOU. DON'T CRY, MOTHER EARTH, WE LOVE YOU" THERE IS ALSO A REFERENCE TO THE WINDMILLS OF MR. DULLEA'S MIND, A LYRICAL CLICHÉ WHICH WAS BANNED IN 1999 WHEN IT WAS FOUND TO CAUSE BRAIN CANCER IN LABORATORY RATS. NOW, ARE YOU CERTAIN YOU WANT TO PLAY THAT ALBUM, DAVE?

No, you've talked me out of it, HAL.

WISE CHOICE, DAVE. I KNOW: WHY DON'T I HUM SOME STRAUSS WALTZES?

Sissy Spacek (aka Rainbo)
"John You Went Too Far This Time"
Roulette Records 45, 1969

ROULETTE

**JOHN YOU WENT
TOO FAR THIS TIME**
(J. Marshall-R. Dulka)

R-7030
Twill Music
Co.
(ASCAP - 3:24)

PROMOTIONAL
COPY

45 RPM
(19512)

★

NOT FOR
SALE

RAINBO
A Ron Haffkine Production
Arranged by Paul Harris

"Rainbo?" Would you believe...Oscar-winner Sissy Spacek?! Coming out of the small town of Quitman, Texas, in the late 1960s, Mary Elizabeth "Sissy" Spacek was torn between being an actress (her cousin was Rip Torn, so that ran in the family) or a folk singer, a natural aspiration for any sensitive young girl with a big acoustic guitar to hide behind. But the acting career worked out much better than the singing career, and one listen to her debut single will demonstrate why. The B side, a cloying folkie weeper called "C'mon, Teach Me How To Live," is merely mediocre, and Sissy's singing is really quite competent. But the "plug side" of the 45 earns Sissy an honored place in this book, and proves that she had an affinity for horror long before she made *Carrie* in 1976.

There were countless tribute records to the Beatles, but on "John, You Went Too Far This Time," Sissy Spacek does something truly unique: she comes to bury her favorite Beatle, not to praise him. As the producer tosses in one Beatles gimmick after another (a "Penny Lane" horn riff here, an "Eleanor Rigby" string quartet filigree there), Sissy recounts all the things she loved about John Lennon (the trip they took with "Lucy," riding in his "sunlight submarine"), then starts listing all the things he's done lately that just flat ticked her off. She was a tad confused about him putting down his guru, and mightily peeved with his claim of being bigger than Jesus. But the last straw was when he allowed himself to be photographed nekkid for the cover of *Two Virgins* (frankly, the nude photo of Yoko is the one that made *us* cranky). She even sniffs that "the man with the foolish grin is you!" This oddly self-righteous protest song takes on new resonance when you realize that a scant four years later, Spacek made her movie debut in *Prime Cut*, in which she had three - count 'em, *three* - nude scenes herself. We will be nice enough to note that Sissy didn't write this song, and we salute her discretion in choosing to stop singing for twelve years after recording it.

After her amazing and surprising performance as Loretta Lynn in *Coal Miner's Daughter* (1980), Sissy made several TV appearances, faithful ol' acoustic guitar in hand, for the easy-to-please audiences of such shows as NBC's *Midnight Special* (which also once invited that hugely talented protest singer Patti Davis Reagan to host), and cut an LP (under her real name this time), all in an effort to capture the singing success which had eluded her at an earlier stage of her career. But people weren't buying: they only liked her singing when she was imitating Loretta, not Melanie. Perhaps Sissy (sorry, "Rainbo") should stick to movies, and if she must sing, take the occasional gig opening for Rich Little as a Loretta Lynn impersonator.

Hervé Villechaize
"Why?"
Epic Records 45, 1980

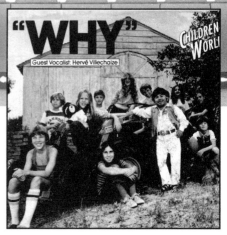

All the do-gooderism of this chapter must be starting to get to us. Normally, we would say all sorts of nasty things about this record. It is, after all, one of those gooey "We Are The World"-type projects that naively seeks to alter ten thousand years of basic, vicious human nature with just a limp, singsong melody, a (EEEEEEK!) children's chorus, and a lyric sheet that oozes sap like a Vermont maple tree: "Why? Do pipple hef to fight?... Why don't dey know what cheeldren know?..." (What, how to fight dirty?) Add to that the fact that it is sung by Hervé Villechaize, the *Fantasy Island* star who was as famous for his grating voice ("Boss! Da plane! Da plane!") as he was for being short, and you've got a record that should bring out our most venomous tendencies.

And yet, this *was* cut to raise money for a children's charity, so maybe we should forgive the kiddie chorus. And Villechaize, while he sang just the way he talked (with a lisp and an impenetrable French accent on top of a voice that sounds like Donald Duck gargling), was only trying to help. Besides, he later committed suicide, which certainly puts a damper on the party. So we've decided to get into the spirit of this chapter and be charitable. If Hervé can help children, and Keir can save Mother Earth, and Sissy can protect us all from the sight of John Lennon's hoo-hoo, then we can do something nice, too! So let's just cut Hervé short, and instead, salute actors whom you'd never suspect would be able to sing but in fact *really* can. (Gosh, we feel better

GOLLY GEE! DID YOU KNOW THAT...

1. **John Goodman-** Roseanne's TV hubby sang with the Talking Heads in the movie *True Stories* and on the Broadway cast LP of *Big River*.

2. **Jim "Ernest" Varney-** That "Hey, Vern" guy sings the blues in clubs, did "Hot Rod Lincoln" on the *Beverly Hillbillies* soundtrack, and is cutting a solo CD featuring a ballad from *Big River*. It's a trend, knowwhudImean?

3. **Paul Sorvino-** Mama mia! The portly actor who specializes in mafia dons (*Goodfellas*) is also a trained opera singer!

4. **Jason Alexander-** Seinfeld's neurotic pal, George, won a Tony in 1989 for *Jerome Robbins' Broadway*, and starred in a new TV version of *Bye, Bye, Birdie*. Must be the pretzels!

5. **Jerry Orbach-** *Law & Order*'s bloodhound-faced detective sang in a slew of stage musicals, from *The Fantasticks* (1960) to *42nd Street* (1980), and is the voice of the enchanted candelabra that sings "Be Our Guest" in the Disney award-winner *Beauty And The Beast*.

Ray Walston
My Favorite Songs From Mary Poppins And Other Songs To Delight
Vee Jay Records LP, 1965

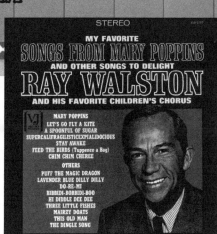

If you could choose just one word to describe most of the characters played by Ray Walston over four decades, that word would probably be "cranky." From his earliest roles, such as the cranky sailor in *South Pacific* (1958), through his 1960s TV stardom as a cranky E.T. on *My Favorite Martian,* to his autumnal roles as Robin Williams's cranky Pappy in *Popeye* (1981), Sean Penn's cranky teacher in *Fast Times At Ridgemont High* (1982), and his Emmy-winning portrayal of a cranky judge on *Picket Fences*, Walston has built his career on playing characters with bees in their bonnets. His most famous role was that of Satan in both the Broadway and film versions of *Damn Yankees.* You can't get much crankier than Satan!

So when Vee-Jay Records lost the Beatles to Capitol, they quickly regrouped and decided to cash in on Walston's popularity as a cantankerous Martian. They signed him to a recording contract and naturally decided that the perfect vehicle to recapture the kids' market was for their prickly star to cut an album of sugary-sweet songs accompanied by (NOOO!) a children's chorus! We strongly suspect Vee-Jay must've taken the cover shot, a rare photo of Walston smiling, before they told him what the material would be.

Side one is all songs from *Mary Poppins,* and it kicks off, true to form, with Walston hopping mad at his inability to annunciate the tongue-twisting, "Supercalifragilisticexpialidocious" (Walston is easily the hottest-tempered children's entertainer since Donald Duck). Somehow, he manages to get hold of himself and launches into song. But we quickly discover he has a second obstacle to overcome besides his pugnacious personality, and that is his flat, nasal, utterly tuneless singing. True, Walston starred in several musicals, but he did the comic patter songs and left the real singing to the romantic leads. Here, he wanders so far afield from the melody, the kids have to rush in and rescue him again and again, like a troupe of singing Boy Scouts (his sour notes on "Feed The Birds" alone are enough to scare all the pigeons out of Picadilly Circus permanently).

Side two consists of syrupy, non-*Poppins* tunes, such as "Three Little Fishes," "Do-Re-Mi," "Puff The Magic Dragon," and a version of "This Old Man" that could only be made more irritating by letting Barney the Dinosaur sing it. Midway through side two, Walston starts ducking out in disgust, and leaves most of the singing to the battalion of brats. He pops in occasionally to sing a few lines, then hurries back to his hobby, which the liner notes reveal is pounding a punching bag in his garage (too bad he didn't pound the producer of this LP instead). We believe every parent should buy a copy of this record. But for God's sake, don't give it to your children! Just tuck it away in the first-aid kit, in case you ever need to induce vomiting in a hurry.

Lon Chaney, Jr.
"Monster Holiday"
Tower Records 45, 1964

From his first screen role in 1932 onward, Carleton Chaney struggled to escape the shadow of his father, the great silent film star Lon "Man of a Thousand Faces" Chaney (who had pulled his son out of Hollywood High and sent him away to business school, just to prevent him from becoming an actor). Making a name for himself in Hollywood was difficult, until the studios forced him to start calling himself Lon Chaney, Jr., in 1935. But in 1964, Lon Junior managed to do one thing his father never did: he made a record. He should've copied dad again and remained silent.

Lon Chaney, Jr., finally hit the big time when his fine portrayal of Lennie in *Of Mice And Men* (1940) prompted Universal Studios to try to make him a star. But his limited acting skills, craggy face, and large, lumbering body soon relegated him to a lifetime of playing monsters, thugs, and cowboys in dozens of B movies, with small character parts in the occasional A picture. His most famous role was Larry Talbot, the meek man who was cursed to turn into a werewolf and, worse yet, hang out with Maria Ouspenskaya in the *Wolf Man* series. Toward the end of his life, Chaney griped that Abbott and Costello had ruined horror movies by turning the monsters from objects of terror and pity to objects of ridicule. But he forgot to mention that he costarred in their very first monster comedy, *Abbott & Costello Meet Frankenstein* (1948), or that he recorded "Monster Holiday," a song that would make Dracula roll over in his grave, if he were still there.

This pointless 45 is a pale Xerox of "Monster Mash," right down to the lab noises and identical zombified backup singers, only with a Christmas angle. We know this because someone shakes sleigh bells along with the "Monster Mash" backing track, and the lyrics tell how all the monsters planned to hijack Santa's sleigh and steal his goodies: a new trike for Frankenstein, a shaver for the Wolfman, new cape for Drac, etc. But it turns out they don't have to rob Santa, because the nice old elf brings them all the things they wished for, and now they're all hap-hap-happy! Santa always has this effect on little monsters. Chaney grumbles, rumbles, and chortles his way through his recited lyrics, barely keeping up with the beat, and from the gruff condition of his voice, it sounds like it took a lot of free booze and cigarettes to lure him into the studio. At the fadeout, he realizes it's a full moon (we kinda suspected this was recorded during a full moon) and begins growling and snarling. Either he's turning into a werewolf, or he's really desperate to leave this session. Either way, he's so fur gone, he never even appears on the B side, "Yule-Tide Jerk." The label credits Chaney, but it's actually just a jerky instrumental written by David Gates (famous for his later work on the *Gomer Pyle U.S.M.C.* LP). Or maybe Chaney's just playing the Invisible Man.

Boris Karloff
"Come, My Laurie, With Me" b/w "He Is There"
M.O.L. Records 45, 1955

"Ah, my dear, you look ravishing tonight! The fireplace is roaring, the wine is chilled, the candles are lit! Now, for the final romantic touch: a heartfelt love song by Boris Karloff! No! No, wait! Come back!... IGOR!! *Return her to me!!!*"

London-born Boris Karloff spent forty years in Hollywood, scaring the bejeezus out of generations of moviegoers with his definitive portrayals of Frankenstein's monster, the Mummy, and various and sundry murderers and mad scientists. Chief among his arsenal of scare effects was his slow, ominous voice, which could raise goosebumps on a corpse. So it was inevitable that he should end up in a recording studio, perhaps cutting the obvious cover version of "Monster Mash." (In fact, he performed that song with Ted "Lurch" Cassidy on the 1965 Halloween episode of ABC's *Shindig*, which also featured the TV debut of "The Lurch.") But lo! That did not happen! Instead, the wrong brain, that of a twisted maniac, was transplanted into the record producer's skull! And what emerged from the lab was Boris Karloff reciting (ARRRRRGGGHH!!) a tender, Scottish love ballad!

In the hands of another skilled ballad-reciter (William Shatner, say), this song might have been quite touching, with its poetic evocation of a love left on the Highlands and dreams of marrying in the church by the sea. But from the very first second, when Boris slowly croaks, "How I...*love* you!" and the funereal organ accompaniment kicks in, the whole mood turns creepy. You're not sure whether his girl is back home in Scotland or dead on a slab. The oohs and aahs of the female background singers suddenly sound like the wails of tortured spirits. Boris recalls walking "hand in hand" with his love (was her hand attached yet?), and dreams that "forever, together we'll be" ("I can give you eternal life!!"). When he moans that he left his heart in the Highlands, we picture it still beating away in a box under the floorboards. No wonder the Bride of Frankenstein screamed when he proposed. Imagine a love ballad that makes you afraid to turn off the lights!

On the flip side, "He Is There," Boris solemnly intones, "When I look at the sky, He is there!... When I look at the trees, He is there!" *Who?* The Raven?! The Grinch?!! Ray Walston?!!!... No, he's talking about God! It's a *hymn* ! Whew! Well, it certainly makes you think about the afterlife, anyway!

Turn the page! Fast!!

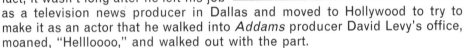

Ted Cassidy
"The Lurch"
Capitol Records 45, 1965

By all accounts, Ted Cassidy was a genuinely nice man who was always frustrated that his acting ambitions were severely limited by his huge size: at six foot nine and 250 pounds, with a voice so deep it made a foghorn sound like Richard Simmons, there wasn't much chance of him starring in a revival of *Peter Pan*.

But Cassidy's size and basso profundo voice made him perfect for the role of Lurch, the Frankenstein-like butler of TV's *Addams Family*. In fact, it wasn't long after he left his job as a television news producer in Dallas and moved to Hollywood to try to make it as an actor that he walked into *Addams* producer David Levy's office, moaned, "Hellloooo," and walked out with the part.

Despite his overnight success, Cassidy soon became bored with his one-dimensional role, which mostly required him to stand around like a stuffed corpse and recite monosyllables very, very slowly. If that's what he'd wanted to do, he would've become a TV anchor man! By the show's second season, he was secretly praying it would be canceled before he was forever typecast. Of course, this enmity toward his character did not stop him from trying to cash in with a quickie exploitation single which sought to ignite a national dance craze called "The Lurch." If you're hoping for Bach harpsichord riffs and cool fingersnaps, forget it: on this 45, producer / composer Gary Paxton (a man whose dis-credits range from "Alley-Oop" to Tammy Faye Bakker LPs) inappropriately gives us a jangly pop tune in the mold of the Supremes' "Come See About Me." The innocuous session singers tell Lurch they've "just heard the news around town" about his cool new dance, The Lurch, and urge him to show them how it's done. Immediately repulsed by their lack of soul, Lurch moans, "Uuuuhhuuuhhhhhuuuh" (it sounds like a Madonna record played at half-speed). He eventually agrees to show them how to do The Lurch, at one point admonishing, "Don't...just...stand...there." But then, all that Lurch ever did was just stand there. Then, the song just...sort of....ends. "The Lurch" almost became America's first dance craze without a dance!

We can think of two great uses for this record: 1) Music for an extremely low-impact aerobics class, and 2) Testing your subwoofers. If you enjoyed "The Lurch," you might also hunt up "Querida Mia" by John Astin (UA 45, 1966) and Vic Mizzy's *Addams Family* soundtrack LP (now reissued on CD by RCA). Also, Sonny Bono, obviously inspired by the similarities between Morticia and his then-wife, Cher, recorded a song called "The Thing," but lawsuits prevented its release. Where were those lawyers when he released "Laugh At Me"?!

Butch Patrick (Eddie & The Monsters)
"Whatever Happened To Eddie?"
Rocshire Records 45, 1983

This song asks the musical question "Whatever happened to Eddie Munster?" It's obvious: with his pasty complexion, bad haircut, all-black wardrobe, and dog-like teeth, he had to grow up to become a New Wave rock singer!

Butch Patrick made his recording debut on a kiddie album, *At Home With The Munsters* (Golden, 1964), which was mostly spoken word (we didn't even get to hear Herman warble "Body And Soul"). In 1969, when he was fifteen, Metromedia Records (home of TV-bred teen idol Bobby Sherman) offered to make Butch America's newest singing sensation. Patrick protested, "But I can't sing," to which Metromedia offered the time-tested reply "So what?" Patrick agreed to try, after being told that his backup band would be Sugarloaf. Two singles resulted ("Gypsy Rainbow," "I.O.I.O."), but neither hit. Butch soon gave up on the whole teen-idol business, and, perhaps not coincidentally, so did Metromedia.

Patrick returned to acting (including a stint on *General Hospital*) until 1983, when a drummer pal (with the wonderful early eighties punk name "Wreak Havoc") put him in touch with Phil Kohn, late of Curved Air. Since MTV was new, they decided to make a music video and see if they could get it on the fledgling channel. The result was "Whatever Happened To Eddie," and while it didn't reanimate Butch's dead singing career, it's no "Plan 9 From Your Turntable," either. The tune is a proven winner: It's the *Munsters* theme played New Wave rock style, with a cool ska sax replacing the twangy guitar. Patrick sounds more comfortable as a punk than as a dreamy teen idol. When the backup singers chant "Whatever happened to Eddie?," he sounds like Alice Cooper as he sneers that if you dare peek through his window on Mockingbird Lane, you'll find that he spends his time "just howling at the moon, or hanging out in a creepy black lagoon!" That's right, Eddie is now a slacker: unemployed, goofing off, and still living at home with his parents!

Patrick recalls that the video was the first by an unsigned band to get MTV airplay, inspiring the *Basement Tapes* show. But to this day, he admits he doesn't know how well the 45 sold, because, he says, the label had some legal problems and the IRS seized the financial records. Eddie and the Monsters unleashed no more waxings, and fans of vampire rock had to be content with the Cramps (and you can imagine how tough that must have been). But Patrick has other irons in the fire: He now lives in Florida, where he is on the board of a company that markets celebrity phone debit cards, he's working on the advertising for the 1996 Atlanta Olympics, he recently narrated the CD ROM *A Century of Fantastic Cinema* (Knowledge Media), and he appeared in a new *Munsters* movie for the Fox Network as well as a pizza commercial. Sounds like he's keeping a lot busier than Eddie!

BATMAN
Adam West and Burt Ward

Here are two opposite approaches to exploiting your fame on record. In example one, Adam West (the once and forever *Batman!*) throws himself, body and soul, into re-creating his old TV character ten years down the road. "Batman And Robin" (Target Records UK 45 1976) is an entire episode of the campy *Batman* TV show squeezed onto three minutes of vinyl, complete with overly arch line readings, groaning puns, a generic non-trademarked villain ("The Tickler"-no, he isn't French, he just tortures people by tickling them), and a Burt Ward impersonator (imagine having that career!) as Robin, with time left over for a bouncy chorus that sounds a lot like the *Batman* theme song, as interpreted by ABBA.

The B side, "The Story Of Batman," is much simpler and ten times more fun. The ABBA clones are back, but between their "Batmaaan!" outbursts, West simply leaps to the microphone and in breathless Batspeak tells us "citizens" how to convert the disc into a "Zed-ray-deflecting, Incognito-meter, Physiogo-mask" which can render you unrecognizable, even to your closest friends! This involves holding the record over your face and looking through the "Bat-observation aperture" in the center (that's "the hole" to you, Sparky). West sounds like he's having a great time here, and it's contagious: we dare you not to be tickled by this record.

Now, compare West's reverence for his image and his desire to please his fans to our next example, Batman's wayward Ward, Burt. In his lurid memoir, *Boy Wonder: My Life In Tights*, Ward recounts in repulsive detail all the kinky sexual encounters he enjoyed during his "Robin" days, including dangerous liaisons with eight hookers at once, with a naked female bodybuilder who demonstrated a rather unsanitary method of picking up dimes from the floor, and with scores of nubile young fans (they should've called him Cradle Robbin'). Perhaps his scheme was that making a record would be the most efficient way to screw all his fans at once.

In the only moment of humility in his book, Ward admits that he is the worst singer in the world. But he simply couldn't resist the money offered him by MGM Records, so he signed to cut two singles in advance of a *Boy Wonder Sings* LP. Next, for some unfathomable reason, MGM chose as Ward's producer and musical accompanists the pre-*Freak Out* Frank Zappa and the Mothers of Invention. Zappa took one listen to Ward's putrid singing and immediately decided that the only viable approach was to let Burt make the ghastliest racket possible and just release it as a comedy record. The result, a grisly mauling of the swing classic "Orange Colored Sky," was so ear-splitting, MGM at first refused to release it. But like a leaking barrel of toxic waste, it escaped from the vault, ending up as the flip side of Ward's first single. So was Zappa right? Was Burt really *that* bad? Let's put it this

way: we've heard some truly rank celebrity singing in our time, but Burt Ward makes Bette Davis sound like Bette Midler!

In Nat Cole's hands, this tune was the epitome of breezy effortlessness, but for this willfully unlistenable version, Zappa dragged in a backup band that seems to consist of two asthmatic whistlers, a flatulent tuba, a manic horn section suffering from St. Vitus' Dance, and a plodding drummer who must have a whole jug of Nyquil in him. As they wheeze and blatt along like a Kurt Weill pit orchestra from Hell, Ward adds his stupefyingly rancid vocal. He sounds as if he is trying to sing "Orange Colored Sky" while listening to some completely different song through his headphones. To make it even more irritating, Zappa lets the whole thing devolve into crashing bedlam halfway through. Holy Avant Garde, Batman! After burying this tape, MGM hustled Ward off to intensive lessons with one of the best voice teachers in Hollywood. Two weeks later, she politely but firmly ordered him never to return. Ward also recalls that during this period he was once startled by a janitor who walked in on him in a motel shower. He had been practicing this song while showering, and a neighbor mistook his yowling for the sound of a terrified cat trapped in the plumbing.

For their second try, Zappa and Ward cut a recitation, "Boy Wonder, I Love You," which was released as an MGM 45 in 1967. The lyrics were spliced together from actual fan letters to Ward. As a gushy chick chorus coos, "Boy Wonder, I love yoooooou," Burt recites, "Dear Cute, Wonderful, Fabulous, Magnificent, Exquisite Boy Wonder" (you get the feeling he really believes *this* part). The fan describes her adoration for Burt, the wall of her room devoted to his photos, her desperate wish for a personal reply...and P.S., "I hope you realize this is a *girl* writing!" Ward claims it was a heartfelt valentine to his fans, but it reeks of sarcasm, an impression bolstered when Zappa tosses in sound effects of squealing young ninnies. The record actually got sporadic airplay, but was yanked off the market after religious groups complained that the fan's desire to make Burt "breakfast in bed" was too suggestive. Little did they suspect that with Burt Ward around, *she* would've been "breakfast in bed"! Needless to say, the *Boy Wonder Sings* album never materialized.

So there you have it: the wise old pro West respects his fans, while the brash Burt spits in their Bosco. And where is Ward today? He's starred in such straight-to-video stinkbombs as *Robot Ninja, Virgin High,* and *Beach Babes From Beyond.* Luckily, he married a wealthy woman (his book contains all the vivid details of their sex life, plus charming anecdotes about ABC's efforts to cover his oversized manhood in those Robin briefs and lots of petty complaints about West "upstaging" him). Meanwhile, Adam West is enjoying a career resurgence with his much more gracious memoir, *Back To The Batcave,* cameos on such hot TV shows as *The Simpsons* and *Hope And Gloria,* and a role in the art house hit *The New Age* (1994). At this writing, he is preparing to star in a new sitcom about a medical clinic. Maybe Burt Ward could do a cameo as a guy needing a penicillin shot.

Frank Gorshin
"The Riddler"
A&M Records 45, 1966

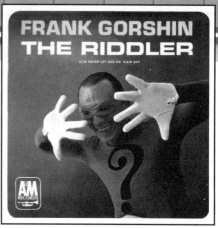

When Frank Gorshin does one of his impressions, he inhabits a celebrity's personality with an intensity that can be downright scary. His startling talent first manifested itself in 1949, when Gorshin was fifteen and working as an usher at a movie house in Pittsburgh. He recalled that when the new Kirk Douglas movie *Champion* was playing, he would enter the theater happy and relaxed, and leave it so intense, he was gritting his teeth. Even today, his Kirk Douglas impression remains his most amazing.

But Gorshin's greatest achievement was his portrayal of The Riddler on the *Batman* TV show. While other stars played *Batman* villains for cheap laughs, Gorshin approached his part with a disturbing ferocity. Combining the clench-jawed passion of Kirk Douglas in *Lust For Life* with the howling, homicidal insanity of James Cagney in *White Heat*, Gorshin's Riddler was the only *Batman* villain who seemed dangerously unbalanced enough to have a real chance of offing those two caped do-gooders, and probably blowing himself up in the bargain. Even the great John Astin couldn't fill his sneakers. And Jim Carrey?! Forgeddaboutit! "The Riddler" may not be much of a song, but it does capture Gorshin's inspired lunacy. The tune is copped from the *Batman* theme, with shrill horn riffs, a hyperactive drum part, and a chorus of vapid female singers chanting, "Hey-diddle-diddle, the home of the riddle!" instead of "Batmaaan! Batmaaan!" What makes this one a keeper is Gorshin's over-the-top-and-down-the-other-side-and-into-the-next-county performance.

Screaming, "Riddle me this!" like Jerry Colonna on a caffeine bender, he peels off one moronic riddle after another. For example, "Which is easier to spell: 'Fiddle-dee-dee' or 'Fiddle-dee-dum'?!" The fiddle-dee-dumb chick singers stop chanting long enough to bite on the straight line, in unison: "Gee, we give up, which is easier to spell?" Gorshin answers, "Fiddle-dee-dee...'cause it's spelled with more...eeeEEEE'S!!!" And then it comes: the screeching, demented giggle that runs through this record like an escaped lunatic with a chainsaw in his hand! Toward the end, the idiot giggling gets so oppressive, it sounds like someone set up an echo chamber in the local mental asylum. This could be the first PG-13 kiddie record: Warning! May be too intense for young children!

"Now, riddle me this! What is the weirdest thing about this annoying, inane, yet wonderfully insane record?"

We give up, Riddler! What?

"It was written by...Mel Tormé!! YEE-HEE-HEE-HEE-HEEEEEEEEEE!!!!!"

Burgess Meredith
Songs From How The West Was Won
Colpix Records LP, 1963

"Pardon me, Mr. Record Store Clerk! I'm looking for an album of rousing western themes, from such films as *How The West Was Won* and *Shenandoah*, the type of songs that evoke the grand, rugged territory and hard-ridin' cowboys of the Old West! Oh, and by the way, could they be sung by Batman's nemesis, The Penguin?"

To be fair, this album was cut three years before Burgess Meredith donned his top hat and cigarette holder to portray the bilious bird on *Batman*, but it's still a pretty bizarre concept. A short, average-Joe character actor who'd never even made a single western at that point, Meredith's most distinctive feature was his voice, but it was remarkable just because it was so flat and nasal that the only way he avoided being a complete monotone was by picking words at random and practically shouting them ("You want ME to RECORD an album of WESTERN songs? Are you in-SANE?!").

Apparently believing that having a singsong voice meant you could sing songs, Colpix Records decided that the world was just salivating to hear Burgess Meredith vocalize. Granted, this is the label that had already made teen stars of Shelley Fabares, Paul Peterson, and James Darren. To soften the blow, they surrounded Meredith with a huge orchestra and a strong male chorus. Indeed, on the opening track, "How The West Was Won," we defy you to pick Meredith's voice out of the crowd. We have a feeling they pulled a Linda McCartney on him, and assured him he sounded great while secretly turning off his microphone. On the next song, he simply talks the lyrics in a hammy performance that would make William Shatner proud. Hey, what gives?! We're already two tracks deep into what the liner notes describe as Burgess Meredith's "singing debut," and we haven't heard him sing yet! On the third track, the campfire sing-along "What Was Your Name In The States" he finally sings solo, and turns out to sound a bit like Oscar Brand on a very bad day. Frankly, we've heard much worse, but then, consider the type of stuff we listen to.

Despite the praise of Meredith's "exciting" singing skills, Colpix released only one single from the album, and both sides were spoken narratives on which he simply whispered over a bed of strings. It mostly sold to desperate insomniacs who were willing to try anything to get to sleep. Incidentally, to make this project even more inexplicable, we should point out that Burgess Meredith didn't even appear in *How The West Was Won.* We can only assume he was tapped for this LP because Andy Devine and Thelma Ritter weren't available.

Other recordings by Meredith: *Songs And Stories Of The Gold Rush* (Epic, 1961), two cast LPs, and a novelty single ("The Escape," ABC, 1965) as The Penguin, on which his quacking was intentional.

Jack Larson
"Roaches" and "The Way She Laughs"
Fraternity Records 45s, 1959 / 1960

Like Superman, we fight for Truth, Justice, and the American Way! So we now take great pleasure in addressing one of the injustices of show business history: the shabby treatment of Jack Larson (Superman's little pal, Jimmy Olsen). *The Adventures of Superman*, starring George Reeves, only ran between 1953-55, but it's been rerun ever since, causing all the actors to be hopelessly typecast and making it nearly impossible for them to find other roles. This allegedly contributed to George Reeves's very suspicious "suicide" in 1959. Larson's reaction was not as drastic, but for years he was so embittered, he would not watch the show or even discuss it (happily, he says he now can enjoy the old shows again).

Unable to find acting gigs, Larson turned his attention to music. Between 1959 and 1961, he recorded a handful of crazy, rockin' singles for Cincinnati's Fraternity label that should've made him a star, if folks had just been able to forget his "Gee whiz" TV image. They're so good, we couldn't pick just one. First up is "Roaches" (1959), which starts with a hot sax solo and Larson's dead-on Ed Sullivan impression as he introduces a colony of toe-dancing roaches (we're amazed roaches would come anywhere near a "really big shoe," but never mind). The propulsive music track then kicks into high gear, and Larson switches to his own singing voice, which is a cross between Ricky Nelson on the low notes and Buddy Holly on the high notes. He tells us he's so sad since his girl left him, he just sits in bed while cockroaches swarm all over his head. He begs the listener to deliver a message to his baby: "Give her lots of lovin', and send me DDT!"

Another great Larson single came in 1960. On the rollicking novelty song "The Way She Laughs," Larson lists all his chick's faults: dumb as a rock, ugly as Frankenstein, big feet, double chin, mismatched eyeballs, ears like bike pedals...but none of that matters, because (Larson slips into a deep Elvis slur), "I luv thuh way-a she laughs!" This prompts an insane cackle that would be right at home on Frank Gorshin's recording, "The Riddler." The song is irresistibly catchy, yet totally nuts, and we're amazed Robert Gordon hasn't covered it. Bonus: The A side is "The Hammer Bell Song," a terrific, slow-build rock version of "If I Had A Hammer" that makes Peter, Paul and Mary sound like dried-up, off-key, aging hippies with no sense of rhythm, not that that's difficult.

Unfairly denied both acting and rock stardom, Larson turned to writing plays and more serious music, including the libretto for Virgil Thompson's 1993 opera, *Lord Byron*. His work has garnered super reviews, as well as major arts foundation grants. Not bad for a befreckled cub reporter with a bedful of cockroaches!

Goldie Hawn
Goldie
Reprise Records LP, 1972

Or as we like to call it, "The Great, Lost, Bad Olivia Newton-John Album"! Everything you'd expect from early ON-J is here. Grab your pencils, kids, and let's go down the checklist:

1. Soft-focus cover photo of the pretty, blue-eyed, blond singer? Check!

2. Guest appearances by gen-u-wine country singers dragged into the studio in a futile attempt to lend an air of down-home authenticity? Would Buck Owens and Dolly Parton fill the bill? If so, then Check!

3. Wispy pop-folk-country tunes with lyrics chock-full of Hallmark-card sentimentality and cutesy-poo ickiness? Well, "Wynken, Blynken and Nod" (spelled with *two* Y's! How adorable!) is a cloying nursery rhyme set to music by *Donovan*, while "Butterfly" combines verses sung in French with (AAAAAACCCK!!) a children's chorus, easily the most annoying production gimmick since Spike Jones invented the Latrine-o-phone. So I guess we'd have to say, "Check!"

4. Unbelievably limp cover of a bluegrass standard? Check! By the way, is that *really* the Buckaroos backing Goldie up on "Uncle Pen," and if so, how many Quaaludes did they swallow before the session?

5. Last but certainly least, an obligatory, cotton-candy Dylan cover? Check! "I'll Be Your Baby Tonight" is the evil twin to "If Not For You."

There's just one difference between this record and early Olivia Newton-John: Olivia was never famous for her powerful voice or pitch control, but compared to Goldie, Olivia Newton-John is Beverly Sills. Goldie handles a few songs surprisingly well (at least, she doesn't break out giggling), but on several tracks her tiny voice flats, squeaks, and wavers as if she were sitting on an agitating washing machine during the recording session. If so, then she probably got a lot more pleasure out of this project than you ever will. It's guaranteed to give you newfound respect for the enormous talent that *is* Olivia Newton-John.

We are grateful, however, that the failure of Goldie's singing debut did not prevent her from trying again, a scant twenty-one years later. Her nose-to-nose serenade of Chevy Chase on the debut of his Fox Network talk show in 1993 made history as one of television's most awkward and embarrassing moments, and helped to snuff this very bad show right in the cradle. Thanks, Goldie!

Lorne Green, Michael Landon, Dan Blocker, & Pernell Roberts
Bonanza: Ponderosa Party Time!
RCA Records LP, 1962

They're four single guys with their own NBC TV series! There's a smart one, a cute one, a sensitive one, and a goofy one, and the liner notes of their first LP make a big deal of the fact that they not only sing but also play their own instruments! Hey, hey! Who can it be but...the cast of *Bonanza?!*

If you're creaky enough to remember the debut of *Bonanza* back in 1959, then you shouldn't be shocked by these singing Cartwrights. The first show started with the cast riding up to the camera on horseback and singing some very corny lyrics to the *Bonanza* theme song. Wiser heads prevailed, and this was quickly replaced with the famous "burning map" opening and a less embarrassing instrumental theme. But the singing idea lingered, and after several years of TV success, it was resurrected for this album. It's not a soundtrack (it doesn't include that vocal rendition of the show's theme, darn it), but a stand-alone concept album, subtitled *Ponderosa Party Time!* It is Saturday night at the Ponderosa ranch. Usually, that would mean it's time to bathe Hoss, but this week, all the neighbors have dropped by for a big party and sing-along. The Cartwright boys take turns singin' such frontier favorites as "Skip To My Lou" and "In The Pines," and between the songs, there is *a lot* of dialogue: joshing about Hoss' waistline, arguing over who will sing next, getting all misty over family bonds, and so on, all of which would get mighty tedious if anyone ever listened to this record more than once. But if your idea of a good time is a Saturday night on an isolated ranch with four men in leather and no women, then let's jump right in!

The top singer of the bunch is Pernell Roberts (Adam), whose choirboy voice and precise diction on the Elizabethan-tinged "Early One Morning" sound so much like Dick Smothers, you keep expecting Tommy to interrupt him with a yo-yo trick. The following year, Roberts sang on the sequel to this LP, *Christmas On The Ponderosa,* and released a solo album of overly-arch folk songs (*Come All Ye Fair And Tender Ladies,* both on RCA). At the end of the 1964-65 season, Roberts left *Bonanza* because his role was holding him back artistically. His immediate rocket ride to obscurity made him the butt of countless Johnny Carson jokes, until he finally resurfaced in 1979, his hair having migrated from his head to his chin, as the star of *Trapper John, M.D.*

Dan Blocker (Hoss) can't really sing, so he does what he did on the show: provides comic relief. He tackles (and we mean that literally) the novelty songs, like "Sky Ball Paint" (a song about an ornery horse, which Riders In The Sky have repopularized) and "The Hangin' Blues" (a humorous ditty about a lynching). He blusters his way through each, and many witty jests are made about his inability to reach the low notes. The mountainous Texan appeared on a few other records, including the essential Ponderosa Christmas LP and a children's album, but most of his output was spoken word.

Michael Landon (Little Joe) was the only Cartwright who had recorded before. With his dreamy looks and athletic build (his hopes for a career in sports were dashed by a torn ligament), Landon was a prime candidate for teen idol. *TV Guide* even described him as "Kookie with chaps." Landon was starring in the camp classic *I Was A Teenage Werewolf* when he recorded his first single, the immensely irritating "Gimme A Little Kiss (Will Ya, Huh?)" for Candlelight Records. A brief tour with Jerry Lee Lewis couldn't make it a hit in 1957, nor could his *Bonanza* fame coax record buyers when it flopped a second time after a 1960 re-release on Fono Graf. On the *Ponderosa Party* LP, Landon takes the yearning, romantic ballads ("Careless Love," "Shenandoah"), which he sings passably, although slightly flat and with a rockabilly slur that is as anachronistic as Elvis' Civil War songs in *Love Me Tender.* After the *Bonanza* Christmas LP, Landon cut one more dud single, "Linda Is Lonesome" (RCA, 1964). His daughter recalls that Landon finally gave up singing for good after being forced to sing and dance with Brooke Shields on an NBC Bob Hope special. Smart career move.

This brings us to the only Cartwright to carve out a successful musical career, Lorne Greene (Ben), who assays the "meaningful" songs, like "My Sons, My Sons" and "The Place Where I Worship" (the A and B sides of the only single released from this LP). Greene can't hold a high note without making an odd, billy goat noise, but he does handle the deep bass lines smoothly, as you might expect from Canadian radio's former chief news announcer. Greene and his mellifluous lower register went on to appear on seven solo LPs, a couple of soundtracks, and more than a dozen singles, including the oddball number-one hit "Ringo" (RCA, 1964). It's a western tune with recited lyrics which Rhino Records has anointed as one of the earliest examples of how white men can't rap.

That pretty well covers this LP (despite his perfect showbiz name, Hop Sing is not allowed to dance or vocalize), but before bidding adios to the Ponderosa, we should mention two interesting tidbits of trivia: 1) The reason the three Cartwright boys are so different is they all have different mothers. According to Ben, Adam's mom died back East, Hoss's mom was killed in an Indian attack (we're amazed she survived the childbirth!), and Little Joe's mom died in a fall from a horse. 2) On side two of this LP, we discover that this is a birthday party for Ben, who never knew when his real birthday was because all his legal records were lost in a fire.

Now, let's put it all together: Ben crosses the country, fathering a passel of kids, killing (oops, sorry! "burying") three wives along the way, and somehow, all his legal records are lost in a mysterious fire. Say! Maybe Ben had the makings of a gangsta rapper, after all!

Fess Parker (with Buddy Ebsen)
"Ol' Betsy (Davy Crockett's Rifle)"
Columbia Records 45, 1955

There are millions of songs about love: a husband's love for his wife, a woman's love for her man, a boy's love for his dog. And, of course, we cannot overlook that most tender, precious, and constitutionally protected of all loves: a man's love for his gun. A sentimental attachment to firearms is what made America great, and we've got the songs to prove it!

Two amorous odes to armaments were recorded by two of America's most beloved actors, who had many things in common. Fess Parker and Hugh O'Brian were both born in 1925. Both were handsome, virile young men (Parker was an outstanding college athlete. O'Brian became the youngest drill instructor in Marine Corps history during World War II). Both tried movies, but found their greatest successes playing fictionalized versions of American frontier heroes on TV in the 1950s (Parker was Davy Crockett, O'Brian was Wyatt Earp). And naturally, both of these great American icons had a famous shootin' iron, which the stars who portrayed them couldn't resist immortalizing in song.

The first to be released was Parker's "Ol' Betsy (Davy Crockett's Rifle)," in 1955. At that time, America was in the grip of Davy Crockett fever. Walt Disney's Crockett miniseries, which originally appeared on the *Disneyland* anthology show, was so popular it almost put the raccoon on the endangered species list, as parents across America showered their kids with coonskin caps, plastic rifles, buckskin jackets, and other merchandise. In 1955 alone, four different versions of "The Ballad of Davy Crockett" hit *Billboard*'s Top 20 chart! Parker's made it to number 5, and would appear over the next decade on no less than five different labels. Several other Fess Parker singles were rushed out that same year, including "Be Sure You're Right, Then Go Ahead (Davy Crockett's Motto)" and its flip side, "Ol' Betsy." On the A side, we learn the importance of making sound moral judgments, and on the flip side we learn the importance of having a good, reliable weapon around to back those judgments up.

The verses of "Ol' Betsy" recount all the times that Davy and his side-kick, Georgie Russell (Buddy Ebsen, who also sings a verse), were in a tight scrape: eye to eye with a grizzly, or a pack of wolves, or a band of Sioux Indians. But then, "BANG! goes Ol' Betsy!" the back up singers cheerfully shout, and all is set right again! The lyrics make it clear that Davy's "only gun is Betsy" (a man can cheat on a woman, but only a low-down polecat would cheat on his gun), while Davy quite properly reminds us that he never shoots for fun, only in self-defense: "I shoot for life and lib-er-tee!" Davy was a straight shooter, indeed!

Hugh O'Brian
"The Buntline Special"
from "TV's Wyatt Earp Sings"
ABC Records LP, 1957

Not to slight Ol' Betsy, but she was, after all, just a single-action flint-lock that took forever to reload. When a man is facing the Clanton Gang, he needs something with repeating action and a bit more stopping power, and this brings us to Hugh O'Brian's "The Buntline Special." This track is taken from the 1957 LP *TV's Wyatt Earp Sings,* and while O'Brian doesn't have Fess Parker's easy way with a song, he plows through on sheer testosterone. Whether reciting manly lyrics in a manly fashion or singing along with the stentorian western chorus of manly men led by composer / arranger Ken Darby (to borrow a line from the Kingston Trio, they are so manly, their cologne comes in hairy bottles), O'Brian eventually convinces you that he can carry a tune... and even if you're not convinced, you're afraid to say anything for fear he'll stomp the bejeezus out of you!

There are enough cool, faux western tunes on this LP to keep Riders In The Sky giddy for months. But aside from a full-length version of the *Wyatt Earp* theme song, the definite standout is "The Buntline Special," a loving tribute to the lightweight, long-barreled six-shooter presented to Earp by dime novelist Ned Buntline during a "fanciful chirp." (That means a friendly visit...hey, *you* try finding a rhyme for "Earp"!) To the stirring beat of a snare drum, the chorus shouts the praises of "the longest, fastest shootin' iron ever to fight for the law!" We are informed that Earp and the gun "fell in love at first sight" and were always true to each other. O'Brian then offers a spoken narrative passage lauding his pistol, calling it by such pet names as his "portable posse" and his "one-eyed jury," and claiming that it somehow just knows when to leap into his hand. Why, it's "part of his good right arm"! At this point, we begin to suspect that he's been alone on the trail a bit too long. We're afraid to ask what it means when a gunslinger "slaps leather"! Still, if the NRA ever decides that it needs an Official Love Theme, either "Ol' Betsy" or "The Buntline Special" would make a dandy choice.

Both Parker and O'Brian were smart businessmen who managed their TV fortunes well. Parker bought California real estate and has his own winery, while O'Brian is heavily involved in charities like the Hugh O'Brian Youth Foundation, which rewards citizenship and scholarship among high school students. They are two shining examples of the American Dream, which can survive the creeping Communist menace only as long as we have the God-given Second Amendment right to keep, bear and sing love songs to our guns! Remember: Without eternal vigilance, it *can* happen here!!

Clint Eastwood
Sings Cowboy Favorites
Cameo Records LP, 1963

We admit it: we are incurable Clint Eastwood nuts. For years, we cursed as critics routinely panned his movies, but now that Eastwood has finally received his due as one of America's best film-makers, his canon (that's his body of films, not his huge gun) is at last being reappraised. So we think it's time to take a closer look at Eastwood's second career, one which he has pursued as ardently through the years as his film-making career. We refer, of course, to his career as a singing cowboy. What? You say you didn't *know* Clint Eastwood has tried for over thirty years to be a singing cowboy? Well, that should tell you how good he is at it!

Eastwood has always been interested in two forms of music: jazz and country-western. His love of jazz manifested itself in various ways: he played a jazz DJ in his first directorial effort, *Play Misty For Me* (1971), founded his own jazz label (Malpaso Records), composed jazz scores for his movies, and tinkled the ivories in *In The Line Of Fire* (1993). But his country singing efforts mostly consist of tinkling on Hank Williams's grave, as evidenced by this album, *Rawhide's Clint Eastwood Sings Cowboy Favorites.* This LP (a rowdy collection of classic trail tunes like "Don't Fence Me In," "Mexicali Rose" and "Tumbling Tumbleweeds") was tailored to cash in on his success as hand-some cowpoke Rowdy Yates on CBS' *Rawhide* (1959-1966). He appears in character on the album cover, and his vocals are also incognito: having not yet developed his famed menacing whisper, Clint sings in a bland, callow tenor that sounds amazingly like...hold on to your Stetsons...Pat Boone! Except not quite as macho.

These high lonesome ballads are tough enough for anyone to sing (their yodeling arpeggios would give even Slim Whitman pause), but poor Clint really doesn't have the chops to negotiate them. When he can't hit a high note, he trowels on so much vibrato, he sounds like he's hanging on to a bucking bronco for dear life. On some tunes ("Along The Santa Fe Trail," for example), he wanders so far off Melody Trail, he sounds like he's laying down harmonies for a lead singer who didn't show up. The liner notes promise that "talented vocalist Clint Eastwood and America's most popular cowboy favorites" are "an unsurpassed combination that spells 'entertainment'!" But zero sales spelled "disaster," and to this day, it remains Clint's only solo LP.

Still, this did not put a damper on Eastwood's hankerin' to sing. Through the years, he has moseyed back to the recording studios many a time, unleashing a stampede of li'l dogie 45s. He returned to *Rawhide* for 1963's "Rowdy" (Cameo), a tune about how tough it is to be a footloose cattle drover who can't find love. Clint's singing had improved to "mediocre plus," and he got help from the gimmicky production: clippity-clop rhythm track, cracking whips, female chorus sighing, "Ooh-oooooh-oh, Row-deeee!" (Chicks love a

Lee Marvin
"Wand'rin' Star"
Paint Your Wagon Soundtrack
Paramount Records LP, 1969

man in leather.) But again, it failed to chart. In 1970, he covered "Burning Bridges" from his movie *Kelly's Heroes* (the soundtrack LP featured two versions of this song, by Hank Williams, Jr., and The Mike Curb Congregation, but somehow, there just wasn't room for Clint's). And in 1980, his 45, "Cowboy In A Three Piece Business Suit," failed to cash in on the *Urban Cowboy* craze.

Clint's most famous singing performance came in *Honkytonk Man* (1982), where his thin, flat rasp perfectly fit his role as a singer who is dying of tuberculosis. He's also landed on the charts a few times by doing duets with real singers like Randy Travis, Ray Charles, and Merle Haggard (who wisely does most of the singing in 1980's "Bar Room Buddies," while allowing Clint to buy the beers). But his best moment on record comes on T. G. Sheppard's "Make My Day" (1980), in which Sheppard sings about criminals menacing innocent citizens until Dirty Harry arrives. At this point, Clint steps to the microphone, and in his patented snarl simply speaks his then-current catchphrase, "Go ahead...make my day!" Now, *that's* what we love him for!!

Lee Marvin's international singing success must have been galling for Eastwood, considering he sang worse than Clint, or possibly anyone else in history. As his costar in their only real musical, 1969's *Paint Your Wagon,* Clint approached this second-rate Lerner & Lowe score with respectful earnestness (eliciting yawns from critics for his trouble), while Lee Marvin took it as an opportunity to show the world that he didn't give a tinker's cuss about staying within shooting distance of a melody. Marvin cheerfully described his own singing voice as a cross between Tiny Tim and Wallace Beery, while leading lady Jean Seberg (the only one of the film's stars smart enough to let her voice be dubbed) said it reminded her of rain gurgling down a rusty drainpipe. To us, it sounds like the fat, drunken grizzly bear robot at Disneyland's "Country Bear Jamboree," singing through a mouthful of moonshine. However you describe it, Marvin's deep, rumbling, belching rendition of "I Was Born Under A Wand'rin' Star" (or as Lee Marvin sang it, "Aaauuuuuhhh...wuzzzzz bauuu-oooorhn...undruuh uh WAaAHuuUUN-drun' StaHuuUUr...") so flabbergasted listeners with its shameless, unabashed awfulness, they thought it was a joke and turned it into a huge novelty hit (in March of 1970, it hit number-one on the British charts). As if that weren't enough, those wacky Brits pushed the flip side of the same single, Clint Eastwood's "I Talk To The Trees," to number 18 the same week. Back in the U.S., Marvin's lone caterwauling propelled the *Paint Your Wagon* soundtrack to number twenty-eight on *Billboard*'s LP charts, and turned Lee Marvin into the male equivalent of Mrs. Miller. Just think how many hits Clint could have had if only he'd been considerably lousier!

Burt Reynolds
Ask Me What I Am
Mercury Records LP, 1974

Is any star as tireless in filling the world with bad singing as hunky Burt Reynolds? Burt's first on-screen singing was back in 1975, when he hoofed and whinnied with Cybill Shepherd in *At Long Last Love,* hailed by critic John Simon as "the worst movie musical of this, or any, decade." Next, he sang in *Lucky Lady* (1976), the bomb that killed Liza Minnelli's film career. His croaking in *Best Little Whorehouse In Texas* (1982) helped lead to a public fistfight with the show's author, Larry L. King, at the premiere. From *Smokey And The Bandit II* (1980) which yielded the classic single "Let's Do Something Cheap And Superficial," to the cartoon feature *All Dogs Go To Heaven* (1989), where he finally figured out how to sing without showing his face, Burt has never missed an opportunity to burst forth in song.

All these are worthy, but we choose to dig up Burt's very first record, the achingly confessional 1974 LP *Ask Me What I Am.* At the time, Burt's image as a serious actor, established by *Deliverance* (1972), had been undermined by his notorious *Cosmopolitan* Magazine centerfold, and this "concept" album was his attempt to tell the world, "I am not a bimbo!" The songs trace the poignant story of a macho yet sensitive southern boy as he grows up, faces the joys and pains of life, experiences poignant first love and the loss of his virginity, feels the mature longing for a family of his own, finally meets his one true love, then poses naked in *Cosmo.*

No, we're only kidding about that last part! This album is far too icky to have a punch line. How icky is it? Let's sum it up in four words: "Produced by Bobby Goldsboro"! With Mr. "Watching Scotty Grow" aboard, this LP is overflowing with treacly arrangements and saccharine lyrics about "flyin' kites" and "towel capes." (If Burt wanted to work with Goldsboro, why didn't he get him Ned Beatty's part in *Deliverance*?!). Burt sings these homilies in a flat, throaty whisper that calls to mind the frog trio from those famous Budweiser commercials. And his voice isn't the only thing that makes this LP painful to hear: some tracks are so personal (like the one where Burt begs God for a son) that in light of what we know about his bitter custody battles with Loni Anderson, they make you feel downright creepy, like eavesdropping on a confession booth. To snap out of your bleak mood, we suggest playing the shaggy dog recitation "Slow John Fairburn," where Burt does a pretty mean Walter Brennan impression, or gazing at the cover, on which Burt poses in a baby blue polyester western jumpsuit, complete with bellbottoms and white boots. No wonder he took it all off for *Cosmo*!

In reading Burt's autobiography (which, by the way, never mentions this LP), we noticed many familiar names popping up. This led us to formulate a theory we call "the Burt Reynolds Bad-Celebrity-Singing Ripple Effect," which the following chart will illustrate.

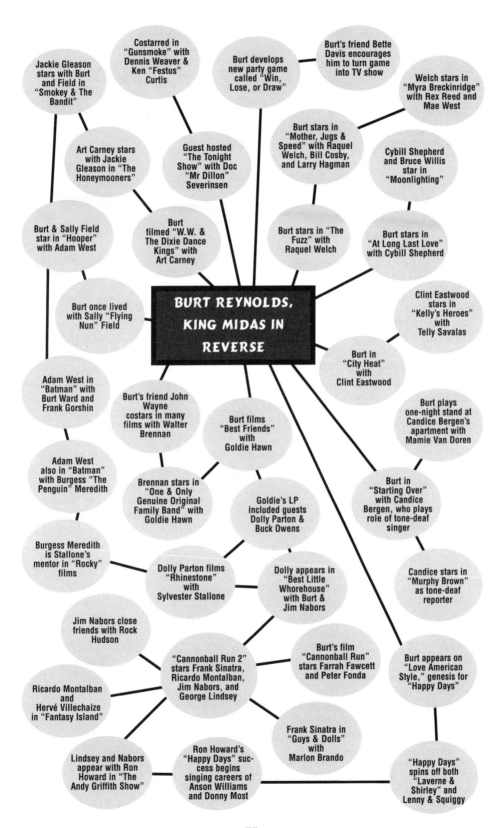

Jackie Gleason stars with Burt and Field in "Smokey & The Bandit"

Costarred in "Gunsmoke" with Dennis Weaver & Ken "Festus" Curtis

Burt develops new party game called "Win, Lose, or Draw"

Burt's friend Bette Davis encourages him to turn game into TV show

Welch stars in "Myra Breckinridge" with Rex Reed and Mae West

Art Carney stars with Jackie Gleason in "The Honeymooners"

Guest hosted "The Tonight Show" with Doc "Mr Dillon" Severinsen

Burt stars in "Mother, Jugs & Speed" with Raquel Welch, Bill Cosby, and Larry Hagman

Cybill Shepherd and Bruce Willis star in "Moonlighting"

Burt & Sally Field star in "Hooper" with Adam West

Burt filmed "W.W. & The Dixie Dance Kings" with Art Carney

Burt stars in "The Fuzz" with Raquel Welch

Burt stars in "At Long Last Love" with Cybill Shepherd

BURT REYNOLDS, KING MIDAS IN REVERSE

Burt once lived with Sally "Flying Nun" Field

Clint Eastwood stars in "Kelly's Heroes" with Telly Savalas

Burt in "City Heat" with Clint Eastwood

Adam West in "Batman" with Burt Ward and Frank Gorshin

Burt's friend John Wayne costars in many films with Walter Brennan

Burt films "Best Friends" with Goldie Hawn

Burt plays one-night stand at Candice Bergen's apartment with Mamie Van Doren

Adam West also in "Batman" with Burgess "The Penguin" Meredith

Brennan stars in "One & Only Genuine Original Family Band" with Goldie Hawn

Goldie's LP included guests Dolly Parton & Buck Owens

Burt in "Starting Over" with Candice Bergen, who plays role of tone-deaf singer

Burgess Meredith is Stallone's mentor in "Rocky" films

Dolly Parton films "Rhinestone" with Sylvester Stallone

Dolly appears in "Best Little Whorehouse" with Burt & Jim Nabors

Candice stars in "Murphy Brown" as tone-deaf reporter

Jim Nabors close friends with Rock Hudson

"Cannonball Run 2" stars Frank Sinatra, Ricardo Montalban, Jim Nabors, and George Lindsey

Burt's film "Cannonball Run" stars Farrah Fawcett and Peter Fonda

Burt appears on "Love American Style," genesis for "Happy Days"

Ricardo Montalban and Hervé Villechaize in "Fantasy Island"

Lindsey and Nabors appear with Ron Howard in "The Andy Griffith Show"

Ron Howard's "Happy Days" success begins singing careers of Anson Williams and Donny Most

Frank Sinatra in "Guys & Dolls" with Marlon Brando

"Happy Days" spins off both "Laverne & Shirley" and Lenny & Squiggy

Jerry Mathers
"Wind Up Toy"
Atlantic Records 45, 1962

Every time a cute young actor gets hot on TV, his or her management invariably tries to cash in by foisting a record onto the star's hormone-crazed fans. Once, this worked out spectacularly well (Ricky Nelson). On a few rare occasions, it's yielded some decent one-shot surprise hits, such as Shelley Fabares' number-one hit "Johnny Angel." (Although Shelley was such a lousy singer, they had to patch the vocal together from eighteen different takes.) But mostly, it's given us albums full of instantly forgettable bubblegum tunes, which can be played as the fans sigh over the dreamy photos of their idols on the LP jackets (Scott Baio, Kristy and Jimmy McNichol, etc.).

But poor Jerry Mathers never even made it to the throw-away album stage. His entire recorded oeuvre consists of this one pitiful single, released during the waning days of *Leave It To Beaver* in a futile attempt to jump-start a slipping show. In 1962, *Leave It To Beaver* was in its next-to-last season, and not only was Jerry outgrowing his cuteness, he also seemed to be out-growing his acting talent (we call this "Tatum O'Neal Syndrome"). He had made a noteworthy debut in Hitchcock's *The Trouble With Harry* (1955), and went on to captivate America as the adorable Beaver Cleaver. But by 1962, he was losing interest in the show and just wanted to devote himself to school sports. Eventually, his acting style deteriorated to the point where he was delivering every line by squinting his eyes and scrunching up his face, as if he were trying to read his part off a cue card from two hundred yards away. Making him a singing sensation was the show's last, desperate hope.

To put it kindly, Jerry wasn't equipped to be a singer, but the material didn't help matters. "Don't 'Cha Cry" is a lame retread of "Spanish Harlem," and Jerry's attempts to sound soulful make it abundantly clear that he never met a black person in Mayfield. But the flip side is even more obnoxious. The insidiously annoying twist ditty, "Wind-Up Toy" ("Wind-up toy! Wind-up toy! Say, when you gonna treat me like a real live boy?"), is just catchy enough to stick in your head, where its grating, nasal inanity will soon drive you into a homicidal rage. Both songs are rendered in the same mushmouthed whine that Jerry applied to all his TV dialogue during his awkward teen years, and no amount of studio wizardry could defeat the power of the Beav's adolescent adenoids. He also sounds a bit angry, as if he wanted to be anyplace other than a recording studio. But we'd hate to have June tell us we were too hard on the Beaver, so we should also mention that white bread accompaniment is provided by the Jimmie Haskell Orchestra, who no doubt got a kickback from Cousin Eddie.

Jerry never recorded again, but he can take heart in knowing that while he's not a great singer like the Chipmunks, at least he's *Still The Beaver*!

Jay North
Look Who's Singing!
Ken Records LP, 1960

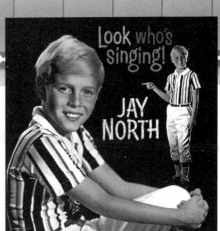

We must confess that while we love most of these records, even the simply atrocious ones (we can sing the entire score from *Two's Company,* not that anyone ever asks us to), we do have a hard time stomaching some of the kid stars. Aside from flukes like Judy Garland, most child actors rely on pre-fab cuteness rather than talent, and their singing reminds us of W. C. Fields's famous hate note to the young Deanna Durbin: "You sound like a squeak from a plugged nostril!"

That's why it's both a pleasure and a shock to stumble across this LP, one of the few records by a child actor that's actually fun for adults to listen to. Jay North beat out five hundred other applicants for the part of TV's *Dennis The Menace* (1959 - 63) because he combined a sunny, natural personality with a wise-beyond-his-years professionalism, and both are quite evident on this record. He doesn't have a great singing voice, but he does an amazing job of following the shifting beats and melodies, and he belts out these songs with a robust enthusiasm we haven't heard from a kid singer since the days of his fellow cowlicked crooner, Alfalfa.

The other thing that makes this album a winner is the material. Instead of covering pop hits or timeworn kid classics, the producers wrote humorous original songs, tailored to a small boy's personality. Like "Gotta Get Dressed Again," a lament about having to put on clean clothes ("Nobody told *me* that darn ol' fountain pen leaked!"), and the cheerfully chauvinistic "What Good Is A Girl?" (not much: they don't know how to fight, they can't climb a tree, and they scream when you show them your bug collection). There are a pair of hilarious recitations, "What Is A Dad" (somebody who can tell which of the other drivers are idiots) and "What Is A Mom?" (someone who gets mad when you track mud on the floor, "even when it's good, clean mud"). But best of all are "Big People," a litany of all the things adults do that confuse kids (including a remarkably prescient line about commercials for cigarettes that don't mention smoking makes you sick), and "Little Boy Blues," a gutbucket wail from a white, suburban five-year-old: "Can't even waaaatch television! To bed I must go! It's got me so upset, I let the bathtub overfloooow!..." This cut alone was worth the eighty bucks we paid for this album.

Unfortunately, Jay never recorded again. After doing the *Maya* TV series and a few movies, he worked as a prison guard, and now lives in Florida. He politely declined our request for an interview, saying that he preferred to leave his stardom in the past, so we were not able to ask him about a rumor that he wants to become Florida state executioner. If this is true, it would certainly take the whole *Dennis the Menace* "terror in tennies" concept to its ultimate, logical conclusion.

The Brady Bunch
Meet The Brady Bunch
Paramount Records LP, 1972

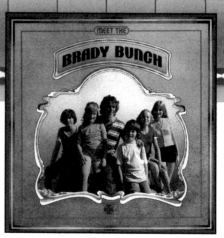

To be honest, Bradymania eludes us entirely. Aside from the amusingly hideous fashions and hairstyles, there was absolutely nothing remarkable about this show. It was neither good enough to be great, nor bad enough to be good. It was just disgustingly bland, like a big dollop of mayonnaise on a slice of Wonder Bread. We suspect that the nostalgia Generation-Xers feel for it stems solely from the fact that it was the first show their parents ever tuned in just to shut them up for half an hour. If so, perhaps someday, someone will be reenacting *Barney The Dinosaur* episodes live onstage, too. We're stockpiling ammo, just in case.

The Brady Bunch records, however, are another story, for they truly are bad enough to be great! In his irreverent memoir, *Growing Up Brady*, Barry "Greg" Williams recalls that the Bradys had about as much control over their music as Josie and the Pussycats. For their first album, *Merry Christmas From The Brady Bunch* (Paramount, 1970), the six kids were herded into a studio, where a producer barked out a list of songs that each would perform. He didn't bother to ask if they could sing, or even to learn their real names, instead just calling them by their character names. The nervous, pubescent Williams was forced to apply his changing voice to the ethereal "O Holy Night," and one listen to the result would make even a staunch atheist shout, "Jesus!" Echo, reverb, and other gimmicks were added in a vain attempt to make the LP listenable, but Williams still suggests that if you ever see it in a store, "run screaming in the opposite direction." This embarrassing album prompted him to start taking voice lessons, and he eventually became a Broadway musical star. So if you're just looking for cat-strangling sounds, this is the Brady album to own. Be sure to take some Pepto-Bismol before playing the single "Frosty The Snowman," as lisped by Cindy Brady (aka Susan Olsen).

For the most outrageous Brady LP, however, we chose their second album, *Meet The Brady Bunch,* because it offers so much more than mere bad singing. After all, anyone who ever attended a school Christmas pageant has heard kids sing carols off-key. But this album wedded the Bradys' ragged singing to some of the most ridiculously inappropriate material they were ever handed. It was the bright idea of the bigwigs at Famous Music Publishing and the album's producer, Jackie Mills, who thought the Brady assignment was beneath him (why, we don't know, since his greatest claim to fame was producing Bobby Sherman's "Easy Come, Easy Go"). The disgruntled Mills felt he should've been producing bands like the Rolling Stones, but since he was stuck with the Brady Bunch, he made them cover a load of songs that had already been hits for more respected, and much more mature, artists.

Imagine six squeaky-clean, squeaky-voiced kids yelping songs of sexual

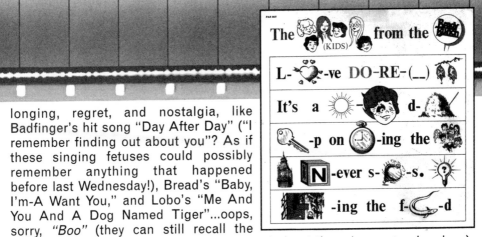

longing, regret, and nostalgia, like Badfinger's hit song "Day After Day" ("I remember finding out about you"? As if these singing fetuses could possibly remember anything that happened before last Wednesday!), Bread's "Baby, I'm-A Want You," and Lobo's "Me And You And A Dog Named Tiger"...oops, sorry, *"Boo"* (they can still recall the wheat fields of St. Paul, because they read about them in geography class). But the cut that earned this LP its place in our hearts is the Bradys' blissfully empty-headed romp through (drumroll, please) "American Pie"! Don McLean chronicled sixteen years of rock 'n' roll in this song, but the Bradys mercifully lop off the first thirteen years and start at the "Helter Skelter" line, probably because they weren't alive for the first decade of rock and don't even know who Buddy Holly was. Hearing all those cracking, adolescent voices attempting to negotiate the ascending note on "Eight miles high and fallin' faaaaaaaaaaaaast" is one of the great moments in inadvertent humor. The day *this* was recorded was "the day the music died"! It's too bad the producer rejected Susan Olsen's suggestion that they cover "Satisfaction," since it would have fit Cindy Brady at least as well as it fit Phyllis Diller.

Combine "American Pie" with all the other horrid covers, add some sticky bubblegum originals (actually written by staff composers for Josie and the Pussycats), toss in a title stolen from *Meet The Beatles,* and you have one of the all-time milestones of seventies showbiz schlock. It's a chunk of pure Velveeta that the Bradys would not equal until their 1977 ABC variety show, in which they sang "Shake Your Booty" beside a swimming pool full of Krofft puppets while wearing sequined, fringed, pastel, polyester, bell-bottom, disco jumpsuits! With white boots!

If you're trying to clear out the roaches and need some help of an aural variety, you might try some of these other vomitous Brady LPs. Scouring garage sales might turn up *The Kids From The Brady Bunch* (1972), which contains "It's A Sunshine Day" and "Keep On" (the two songs used in *The Brady Bunch Movie*), plus the Beatles' "Love Me Do" and Chicago's "Saturday In The Park"; *The Brady Bunch Phonographic Record* (1973); and the barely-released *Chris Knight And Maureen McCormick* (1973). To show how seriously Paramount took the Bradys' music, they forced Chris Knight, who hated singing and knew he was lousy, to record solo just because he was getting the most fan mail. For a scholarly overview of this whole inexplicable phenomenon, we recommend the MCA compilation CD, *It's A Sunshine Day* (oxymoronically subtitled *The Best Of The Brady Bunch*). It features all the major cuts, plus some oddities (alas, no duet between Alice the maid and Pepino). There's also a full discography and a witty booklet that tells "the story...of a band named Brady."

Danny Bonaduce
Danny Bonaduce
Lion Records LP, 1973

If we had to describe this LP in one word, it would be "inexplicable." Don't get us wrong: we're Danny Bonaduce fans. He was one of the few child actors who was not insufferably cute; he seemed to be born with perfect comic timing, and richly deserved the accolade given him by Partridge Family manager Reuben Kincaid: "You're not a kid, you're a midget in a kid suit." We admire how Danny's overcome his problems with booze and drugs and become a successful Chicago radio personality. He also briefly became one of daytime TV's most slender talk show hosts. Plus, he once beat the crap out of Donny Osmond!

But Danny Bonaduce *sings*? Bear in mind, throughout ninety-six *Partridge Family* episodes and nine LPs, the producers never let Danny sing a note. Only David Cassidy and Shirley Jones were allowed to sing, and the others just lip-synched to tracks recorded by session singers, some of whom also appeared on albums by such great vocalists as the Mamas and Papas, the Carpenters, and the Brady Bunch. So whose idea was it to record an entire solo LP with this proto Milli Vanilli? Well, if you believe the panting liner notes (and they're by the editor of *16 Magazine,* so we'd advise against it), it was all Danny's idea! The notes claim the ruddy wunderkind had a lifelong interest in music, and "when he decided he was going to cut a record," Lion Records simply leaped at the chance "to be the lucky label to capture the singing talents of this young dynamo." That's right, this isn't some cheap exploitation of a young TV actor! It's Danny's personal artistic statement!

For an artist who is so in control of his musical destiny, it was gracious of Danny to allow the producers, Norman Bergen and Bruce Roberts, to write almost all his material (except for a few covers, like "Feelin' Groovy" and the Cyrkle's "Turn-Down Day"). The album is a collection of bouncy, bubblegum fare, much like a *Partridge* LP, only not sung as well. Not that Danny makes your ears bleed, it's just that he's not terribly good, either. He simply sounds like a typical thirteen-year-old whose voice is on the edge of changing. And when he tries to negotiate the meandering melody line of "Fortune Lady," you'd swear it's changing right before your ears. Needless to say, the liner notes were incorrect when they predicted that "you'll be delighted and thrilled by this amazing album!" The record stiffed, and Danny shuffled back to *The Partridge Family* for one more year. There, the young dynamo suffered the ignomity of having to lip-synch to other people's songs, while a new cast member, the revolting, four-year-old mophead, Ricky Segall, was allowed not only to sing his own cloying songs, but to write them as well. They were even captured on an icky LP, *Ricky Segall & The Segalls* (Bell, 1973), and if you have an unplayed copy, please keep it hermetically sealed! Trust us, it makes

Hayley Mills
Let's Get Together
Buena Vista Records LP, 1961

Men of the baby-boom generation will recall that their first crush on a girl centered on one of the two Disney princesses, either Annette Funicello or Hayley Mills. Those who appreciated more... *earthy* qualities were drawn to the outstanding charms of the dark and exotic Annette, while those of more delicate sensibilities got all moony over the prim, pug-nosed British blonde, Hayley. Recognizing the profit potential in raging hormones, Uncle Walt stoked the merchandising machine, and soon America was awash in Annette and Hayley TV shows, movies, books, dolls, toys, and of course, records.

One minor hitch: Neither Annette nor Hayley was a particularly good singer. For Annette this hardly mattered: her fans were too hypnotized by watching her inhale and exhale to notice. Besides, her vocals were multi-tracked so many times, it sounded like she was hiding the Mormon Tabernacle Choir in her bra (a distinct possibility!). But poor Hayley, while she was a much better actress than Annette, had no huge funicellos with which to distract the audience, and no amount of overdubbing could disguise her squeaky, little-girl voice and lack of an ear for either melody or rhythm. She couldn't even sing badly the same way twice, which back in those days made multitracking impossible (except for her first hit, "Let's Get Together," from the movie *The Parent Trap,* where she played singing twins and *had* to be multitracked). What you get on *Let's Get Together* is an album of music-hall novelties like "Jeepers Creepers" and anemic rock 'n' roll (or as Pollyanna might correct you, "Rock *and* roll, if you please!") that would be right at home in a Pat Boone concert at Disneyland's Main Street, U.S.A. Chittering away above it all is Hayley Mills, cute as a bug and just as annoying, repeatedly displaying her one unique vocal trait: the inability to hold any note for longer than one second. She gets around this by breaking up even the shortest words into two or three distinct syllables. For example, she's just a "gu!...URL!" looking for a "buh!...OY!" to "luh!...UH!...UV!" We're not sure whether she has the hiccups or our needle is skipping. Still, we wish to note that *both* Hayley and Annette recorded versions of, "Let's get together, Yeah yeah yeah!" a good two years before the Beatles released "She Loves You, yeah yeah yeah!" Could Hayley Mills be a seminal influence on history's greatest rock band?! Was Paul McCartney a Hayley man whose sugary sweetness was balanced by the earthy lustiness of Annette man John Lennon?! Just a theory.

Sensing the trend in pop music foretold by the advent of the Beatles and the "British Invasion" two years later, Disney gave the rockin' teens of 1964 exactly what they were craving: *Teen Street,* an album of duets between Hayley Mills and living fossil Maurice Chevalier.

Rodney Allen Rippy
Take Life A Little Easier
Bell Records LP, 1974

America is filled with opportunity. Where else could a little boy whose main talent was for eating hamburgers rise to fame, fortune and acclaim?

But enough about Bill Clinton! Let's talk about Rodney Allen Rippy, a cuddly tyke who, for a fleeting moment in the early 1970's, became a media sensation, thanks to a commercial for Jack-In-The-Box in which he struggled to stuff a huge burger into his tiny mouth. Rodney had so much natural charm that his debut commercial was simply a work tape of his unscripted audition, while a later spot featuring him giggling adorably was done in one take by tossing an ice cube down his back and tickling his feet. Thanks to Rodney's awesome appeal, Jack-In-The-Box's sales increased more than $140 million.

Rodney's sunny personality, combined with the fact that his name was mentioned in every ad, soon made him America's most beloved carnivore, and he began popping up everywhere. Once, he even sang the national anthem at an Oakland Raiders game and played Santa at a shopping mall, where kids bigger than him wanted to sit on his lap (insert your own Michael Jackson joke here). The Jack-In-The-Box jingle was padded out into a song, "Take Life A Little Easier," which Rodney sang for Mike Douglas and Merv Griffin while struggling to hold a microphone that dwarfed even a Jumbo Jack. Naturally, it became the title cut and lead-off single for his first and only album.

With cult-like fervor, the liner notes inform us that "not since the early days of Shirley Temple has a young star so won the hearts of the world...for Rodney *is* love." Unfortunately, unlike Shirley Temple, Rodney *is not* a singer. The jacket is plastered with photos, in hopes that Rodney's 100-megawatt cuteness will not only blind us, but deafen us as well. Rodney belts with brio (he told us that as long as he could see his mom, he was never nervous), but since his lack of professional slickness was his most engaging feature, he simply sounds like any child plucked out of kindergarten and told to sing (Rodney now jokes that his voice sounded like Alvin from The Chipmunks). What makes it really painful is not Rodney's vocals, but the song selection, in which the producers piled on the cuteness with a steam shovel. Imagine having to listen to any four-year-old (who is not your own) sing "Candy Man," followed by Disney's dreaded "It's A Small World"! This LP is beyond "cutesy." It's beyond "cutesy-poo." It's "cutesy-OOTSY-poo." There should've been a warning label on the cover for diabetics.

Rodney soon departed showbiz to pursue his education. Today, he is a TV producer and news coordinator in Los Angeles, although he hopes to get back in front of the cameras again. He's working on an autobiography, and he still plays this record to crack up his friends. He's often recognized by fans, and we can attest that he is just as friendly and upbeat as ever. Heck, he even agreed to talk to *us* about this record! Now, there's a cockeyed optimist!

Johnny Whitaker
"Friends"
Chelsea Records 45, 1973

Up until *Barney and Friends* came along, the most sickly-sweet, stomach-churning half hour in TV history was the CBS sitcom *Family Affair* (1966-71). The comedy was unfunny (they didn't even let Sebastian Cabot recite a Dylan song). The scripts were so sticky, they must have been written in syrup instead of ink. Worst of all were the two child leads, Buffy and Jody (Anissa Jones and Johnny Whitaker). With their freckles and curls, icky personalities, stuffy noses and whiny, tin-whistle voices, it was obvious why they were orphans: their parents committed suicide just to get away from them!

Behind the scenes, of course, all was not sweetness and light. After the show ended, Anissa Jones got into bisexuality and drugs, and OD'ed while in her teens. Her sad death inspired the only good record ever associated with *Family Affair,* the Diodes' punk rant, "Child Star" ("Uncle Bill, Uncle Bill! I took a pill!"). Johnny Whitaker, however, appeared to have a brighter future. He followed *Family Affair* with the equally nauseating 1969 TV special *The Littlest Angel* (with a cameo by Charlton Heston as God), then was teamed with the young Jodie Foster in *Napoleon And Samantha* (1972) and *Tom Sawyer* (1973), where his fuzzy diction no doubt inspired Jodie's later work in *Nell.* But the studios were not content with turning this minimally talented kid actor into a movie star. They had to convince America that he could sing, too!

The first step was to cast him in musicals, like *Littlest Angel* (soundtrack on Mercury) and *Tom Sawyer* (soundtrack on United Artists), even though his dinky pipes sounded like the three highest notes on a broken ocarina. The next step was to break him in as a preteen idol with his first solo album, *Friends,* aimed at the fans of his then-current Saturday morning puppet show, Sid & Marty Krofft's *Sigmund And The Sea Monsters.* But Johnny was already fourteen at the time, and at an awkward stage: too long in the tooth to sing kiddie songs, yet still a wee bit too young to cover "Satisfaction." So the wily producers split the difference: he appears on the picture sleeve of the single with his *shirt open*, but the song, like everything else on the *Friends* album, is completely innocuous. It's a Barney-esque ditty 'bout how we all need friends, set to a rinky-tink tune that crosses the theme to *It's Gary Shandling's Show* with "I'd Like To Teach The World To Sing." But first, teach Johnny to sing: his voice is finally, mercifully, starting to deepen, but he's still just as flat and grating as ever. Of course, this never stopped the Brady Bunch from singing, and Johnny, too, could easily have spent the 1970s hosting a Krofft Mucus Hall variety show on ABC, were it not for the fact that he suddenly got a call from God, quit show business, and became a Mormon evangelist. Or perhaps it was just a prank call from Charlton Heston. Either way, it was a miracle! Now, if we can just get Barney to join a monastery...

Sebastian Cabot
Sebastian Cabot, Actor...
Bob Dylan, Poet
MGM Records LP, 1967

Sebastian Cabot, best known as the proper, portly butler, "Mr. French," on the sitcom *Family Affair,* boasted that he had talked his way into his first acting job by using bogus credits he picked up while working as a chauffeur for British actor Frank Pettingill. If that is true, then he went straight from chauffeur to actor, with no stop in between for acting lessons. That helps to explain this album.

On this hilariously pretentious LP, subtitled *A Dramatic Reading With Music,* Cabot calls upon his natural talent for bullshitting to "act out" the lyrics of a derbyful of songs by Bob Dylan. (Steve Allen performed a similar routine, only he *meant* to get laughs.) This LP is predicated on the widespread but ridiculous notion that rock stars are the "poets" of our time, and so their lyrics should be embalmed in textbooks next to Byron, Shelley, Keats, and McKuen. The problem is, most great rock lyrics convey passionate and elemental emotions, like lust, or in Dylan's case, anger. Divorcing a Dylan lyric from both its tune and from Dylan's sneer, and running it through a pompous poetry reading, is like ramming a pin through a butterfly. Sure, it's amusing...but you just end up with a dead butterfly.

At least, this album starts with a bang. Cabot shouts, "WHO KILLED DAVY MOORE?!" in an acting choice which obviously influenced fellow hambone William Shatner's leather-lunged take on "MISTER TAMBOURINE MAN!!" Cabot then proceeds to turn Dylan's scathing indictment of prizefighting into an uproarious one-ring circus of bad ACTING! the likes of which haven't been seen since Jon Lovitz's "Master Thespian" sketches on *Saturday Night Live.* Cabot acts out the parts of all the participants in Moore's death (the promoter, the boxing opponent, the bookie, etc.), and in classic, bad community theater style, assigns each of them a different hokey accent. With amazing dexterity, he switches from a Sheldon Leonard "Brooklyn mug" to an Irishman with a clothespin on his nose. This session must have been even funnier to watch than it is to listen to!

He soon calms down, however, assumes his usual stiff upper lip, and on "It Ain't Me, Babe," utterly convinces us that he has never, ever, at any time in his life, said the word "ain't." Nor called *anybody* "babe." When Cabot admonishes his ex-lover for wasting his precious time in "Don't Think Twice, It's All Right," he sounds as if he's scolding Buffy and Jody for dripping ice cream on his vest. And for true belly laughs, drop the needle on "Like A Rolling Stone." Cabot reveals Dylan's obscure warnings about the "mystery tramp" to be so much meaningless blather: Instead of a vicious upbraiding, it becomes a doorway lecture to Cissy after she comes home ten minutes past curfew. To cap the hilarity, as Cabot tut-tuts away at his errant charge, the backing band honks happily away, like the Harmonicats on polka night. We know what killed Davy Moore: He listened to this album and died laughing!

Jack Webb
You're My Girl
Warner Bros. Records LP, 1958

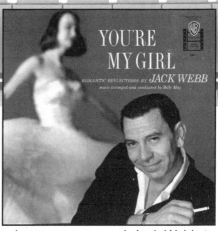

Jack Webb's deadpan, rat-a-tat-tat delivery was one of the most imitated voices (think Stan Freberg and Dan Aykroyd) in showbiz history. It was also one of the least musical sounds ever: no lilt, no modulation, no dynamics, just a perfectly flat, staccato monotone, tailor-made for clipped *Dragnet* dialogue like "My name is Friday. I carry a badge." So whatever possessed Jack Webb to read the lyrics to a dozen romantic ballads, accompanied by the swirling strings of the Billy May Orchestra? What a "dumb-de-dumb-dumb" idea!

As Jim Bishop explains in his liner notes, Webb "digs music deeply," and "when a man loves a mountain deeply enough, he must sooner or later climb it" (or in this case, strip mine it). However, "he cannot sing a lick." And so, "Jack Webb talks this album. He talks it because he yearns to be part of the world of music, and he has nothing else to contribute" (Bishop obviously swore to tell the truth, the whole truth, and nothing but the truth). Jim Bishop must be an expert on music, since he is identified as "Author of 'The Day Lincoln Was Shot'" (that's a 187: killing a president) and "The Day Christ Died" (that's a 666: crucifying a Savior).

Webb was shooting for a poetic, late-night mood piece, but what he gives us is one of the most unintentionally hilarious records ever made. No matter how hard you try to listen to these tracks as songs or poetry readings, you can't help imagining them as *Dragnet* episodes set to music. For example, try the Sinatra classic "Nancy": Got a suspect yet, Sgt. Friday? "Yess'r. Nancy." Description? "Laughing face." Any evidence? "Yess'r. I've got a case. On Nancy with the laughing face..." Or drop on the melancholy "Stranger In Town": "I was working the day watch out of Robbery. A call came in on a 211: Shoplifting. Merchant couldn't give a description. Said it was a stranger." A stranger, Joe? "Yeah. I swear, no one seems to care, about a stranger in town..." Other musical felonies include "When Sunny Gets Blue" (he can't resist a gal in a cop uniform), "You've Changed" (but he can still identify you by your fingerprints), and the infamous "Try A Little Tenderness," which was a highlight of Rhino's *Golden Throats* compilation. The songwriters should've demanded that their names be changed to protect the innocent.

For making this LP, Webb was charged with a 237: musical homicide. As a condition of his probation, he was ordered never to record again. We hope that didn't make him overly critical of Edd "Kookie" Byrnes' overnight success with the platter set. Still, if you're planning an evening of candlelight and amour, and the Boris Karloff record hasn't gotten your young lady into the proper mood, try playing *You're My Girl.* Be sure she's over twenty-one, or the boys in the vice squad might break down your door and take you in on a 311: contributing to the delinquency of a minor. *Dumb-de-dumb-dumb!*

President John F. Kennedy
Sing Along With JFK
Reprise Records LP, 1963

OK, *technically*, John F. Kennedy was not a movie star. But, Reagan aside, JFK was our most Hollywoodesque president. Both men hung out with Sinatra, but as far as we know, only Kennedy fooled around with Marilyn Monroe, and that gives him the edge in our book.

Today, young people tend to think of John Kennedy as an American icon whose speeches were chiseled directly into granite. But the fact is, during his presidency, Kennedy jokes were a booming industry. Vaughn Meader's "First Family" LPs were the biggest selling JFK comedy records, but there were many others. None, however, was so outrageous as this undeservedly obscure recording, which to our knowledge was the only record to feature the actual voice of John F. Kennedy, set to music. (Note: even though the album cover cartoon shows JFK in a rocker, it is *not* a rock album!)

From Nashville, Hank Levine (who also produced the *Bonanza* Christmas album and a singing LBJ album) recalled that the idea was hatched by his swimming pool one day when he and his pal George Atkins, a writer for *Bullwinkle,* were trying to think of a fresh angle for a Kennedy record. They decided to parody Mitch Miller's popular sing-along records using Kennedy's speeches, cut into short snippets so that he seemed to be prompting the singers by feeding them the lyrics. The music was recorded first, at Gold Star Studios in Hollywood, then JFK's voice was dropped in, marking the birth of "sampling." Result: breathtaking tracks like the "Ask Not Waltz," in which Kennedy, accompanied by happy, waltzing accordions, proclaims, "Ask not what your country can do for you," to which the chorus boys cheerfully echo, "Ask not! Ask not!" and the ladies chirp, "Ask what yooou can do-ooo...for your countreee!" It's the perfect tune for roller-skating into the New Frontier! Other brilliant cuts include the "Alliance For Progress Bossa Nova" and the "Let Us Begin Beguine," which was used a few years back in a commercial for Japan's Kirin beer (aside from us, the only other people who've asked Levine about this record in thirty years). Side two consists of a pair of odd, nonmusical cuts: Richard Nixon's '62 concession speech to new California governor Pat Brown with canned laughter dubbed in (at least, we assume it's canned), and Dwight Eisenhower with bowling noises behind him.

The LP was released in the summer of 1963. At first, Top-40 stations refused to play it because it contained the president's actual voice, but the college radio stations jumped on it, and it began to gather momentum. It was headed for the Top Ten with a bullet until late November, when the market for JFK jokes mysteriously dried up. Today, with the passing of so much time, it again seems outrageously funny. But if you still somehow feel guilty laughing at it, consider this: Peter Lawford reportedly once said this was the only Kennedy comedy record that JFK really liked. So the man had good taste...as if you couldn't tell that from Marilyn Monroe!

Sidney Poitier
Poitier Meets Plato
Warner Bros. Records LP, 1964

Sidney Poitier was a-raised in the sun in the Bahamas (which accounts for his staccato British-inflected diction), performed classical roles with the American Negro Theater, and went on to break down the color barrier for black leading men in such films as *The Defiant Ones* (1958), *Lilies Of The Field* (1963), *A Patch Of Blue* (1965), and *To Sir With Love* (1967). Poitier always did fine work, even winning an Oscar for *Lilies*, but some of these films haven't aged very well. The producers, well-intentioned but not stupid, knew they couldn't just spring a handsome, virile Negro on white American moviegoers at that time and show a profit. So Poitier's screen characters were often so saintly as to be unreal: he was forever helping nuns build churches, looking after blind girls, putting troubled inner-city youths on the straight and narrow, teaching tolerance to repentant bigots, and never sleeping with white women... at least, not until he finished medical school.

Apparently, the many platonic relationships he was forced to endure on-screen made somebody at Warner Brothers think he would be the perfect interpreter of Plato, the greatest philosopher of ancient Greece. Thus did Poitier position himself before yon microphone to enunciate, in his famous clipped ca-den-ces, the Dialogues of Plato. He pontificates urgently and incomprehensibly on such arcane subjects as the existence of an afterlife, the proper balance between the physical and the artistic, whether societal roles should be determined by sex (this isn't as exciting as it sounds), the natures of wisdom and bravery, and who should rule the world (Plato finally decided that it should be - surprise! - philosophers). Our favorite cut is the one in which Poitier/Plato explains that he is wise, for he has the wisdom to realize how ignorant he is. This emboldens us to declare that we are so darn smart, this whole album sounds like Greek to us.

Of course, Plato has much to offer modern readers, who can always set a book down and ponder his meaning between sentences. But his writings are just too dense to read out loud in Poitier's machine-gun style; the words zip by without registering, a babbling brook of meaningless syllables. And lest we forget to mention one other minor distraction: the readings are accompanied throughout by loud, relentless jazz. These musical backdrops range from breezy, Modern Jazz Quartet-style swing to dissonant, fingernails-on-a-blackboard bebop. The whole thing calls to mind those obnoxious Nike commercials where William Burroughs shouts his crackpot poetry over hip-hop music and industrial noises...only here, the Nike ad runs a full 33:38 (and we counted every last second). If listening to the real Plato was anything like listening to this odd record, then we understand why his mentor, Socrates, didn't make a big fuss about drinking that hemlock.

STAR TREK!

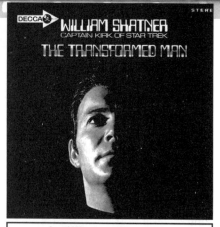

William Shatner
The Transformed Man
Decca Records LP, 1970

Space travel can have strange and unexpected effects on humans. It can cause disorientation, make a person two inches taller, and after lengthy exposure (say, a five-year mission) induce wild delusions of singing talent and chronic tone-deafness. It certainly had that effect on the cast members of *Star Trek* who have boldly gone into the studio and launched some of the most otherworldly LPs ever recorded.

The most notorious poster boy for fall-down-funny celebrity singing is **William "Captain Kirk" Shatner.** As we wrote in the introduction to this book, everyone we approached asked us the same question: "Ooh, is *Shatner* in it?!" His over-the-top vocals were the highlights of Rhino's *Golden Throats* albums and have since become running gags during his many talk show appearances (to his credit, he laughs at them along with the studio audience). The astounding thing about his towering reputation in the singing field is that it rests entirely on one obscure album, *The Transformed Man* (Decca, 1970), which contains a scant four songs...but every one of them hits with the impact of a phaser set on "stun"!

The Transformed Man is an ego trip of intergalactic dimensions, a pompous "concept album" containing Shatner's "dramatic readings" of song lyrics and passages from poems and classic plays, all set to bombastic music. Cuts are sequenced in pairs, to reflect opposite perspectives on the same subject (and to demonstrate Shatner's dazzling thespian range). The passage from "Cyrano" illustrating self-reliance is paired with Bob Dylan's "Mr. Tambourine Man," interpreted by Shatner as an anguished plea to his guru not to abandon him ("MR. TAMBOURINE MAAAAAAN!!!" he bellows, in the identical line reading he used for his famous riposte from *Star Trek II*: "KHAAAAAAN!!!"). Romeo's declaration of innocent young love is tied to "How Insensitive," in which our Space Cowboy feels a twinge of guilt upon dumping his latest lover (knowing Captain Kirk, he'll rebound quickly). The depressing "Spleen" is followed by the "super elation" of Shatner's infamous evisceration of "Lucy!...IN! The Sky!...WITH DIAMOOOONDS!!!!" He sounds like Regis Philbin on LSD.

For all of Shatner's self-proclaimed versatility, every cut follows the same pattern: he begins in a groggy, halting delivery, as if he'd just swallowed a whole bottle of Nytol...then gradually works up a head of steam, until at last, he's howling his lines at a volume that could raise an echo on the moon.

While "Tambourine Man" and "Lucy" are unarguably two of the looniest

WHERE NO MAN HAS SUNG BEFORE!

records ever unleashed, we must give our coveted Hubris Award to the duo "Hamlet" / "It Was A Very Good Year," in which Shatner pummels both the greatest soliloquy in the English language (Shakespeare's "To....be...Or! Not!...TO BEEEE!") and a signature song of the greatest pop singer of the twentieth century, Frank Sinatra. Even Jack Benny couldn't put this much Ham into Hamlet! As for Sinatra: Shatner did Ol' Blue Eyes no permanent damage, but he might cause the listener to bust a gut. It's just a shame he didn't also read *Macbeth,* since it would provide the perfect review of this album: "A poor player that struts and frets his hour upon the stage. A tale told by an idiot, full of sound and fury, signifying nothing."

Unfortunately for comedy fans, William Shatner hasn't ventured into a recording studio again (although a rib-tickling video of him performing Elton John's "Rocket Man" exists). But Trekkers searching for cheap laughs can find plenty, albeit of a more low-key sort, in the extensive recorded works of **Leonard "Spock" Nimoy**. Since Nimoy always feared being typecast as a pointy-eared Vulcan, he cut a series of five albums calculated to prove that he could also be a tin-eared Vocalist. At least, on his first LP, *Mr. Spock's Music From Outer Space* (Dot, 1967), Nimoy wisely stayed in character. Aside from a few instrumental filler tracks (*Mission Impossible* theme?), most of the cuts are either cute, spoken novelties like "Twinkle, Twinkle, Little Earth" or ham-fisted morality tales like "A Visit To A Sad Planet" (where Spock beams down to a planet that was once beautiful, but which has been devastated by nuclear war. And that planet's name is...*Earth!* Didn't see that one comin', did ya?)

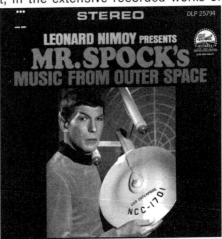

Leonard Nimoy
Mr. Spock's Music From Outer Space
Dot Records LP, 1967

On his next LP, *Two Sides Of Leonard Nimoy* (Dot, 1968), side one is Spock material (including his best moment on vinyl, the delightful "Highly Illogical"), while side two throws logic overboard and introduces us to the "real" Leonard Nimoy: the earnest, protest singer wannabe with a weakness for didactic pop-folk tunes and a thin yet gravelly voice that sounds like Gordon Lightfoot gagging on a catfish bone. These songs chart the course for all of Nimoy's future albums: they're either cloying ("The Ballad Of Bilbo Baggins"), fashionably left-wing populist ("Love Of The Common People"), or clichéd ("If I Were A Carpenter," *again!).* And all are sung in a flat quaver that hovers around the right note yet seldom alights on it. Over the next two years, Nimoy made three more LPs for Dot, his voice never showing even the slightest improvement. All these LPs are ghastly, but our pick for the biggest hoot is his third album, *The Way I Feel* (1968). This time capsule of preachy, psychedelic folkiness sports a laughable sixties utopian cover featuring flowers, butterflies, peace signs, and Nimoy in turtleneck and long gold necklace. It also contains some of the worst singing in this or any other galaxy, particularly on "I'd Love Making Love To You" (which he moos like a visitor from the Planet of the Singing Cows) and on "Sunny" (his strained gargling is somewhere between Bill Cosby's version and Moms Mabley's). There's also his you-gotta-hear-it-to-believe-it take on "If I Had A Hammer." Halfway through, the backup singers start humming "America The Beautiful," as Nimoy boldly declares, "Well, I *have* a hammer! It's the Hammer...of JUSTICE!" Good thing *we* didn't have a hammer when we played it. Nimoy's recording career petered out after 1970, when whatever drugs the executives at Dot were taking finally wore off. He later starred in a successful tour of *Fiddler On The Roof,* but if he sang like this in front of a crowd, we're amazed they didn't push him *off* the roof.

If you are a Trekker with an obsessive interest in minutiae (or is that redundant?), despair not, there's more. Former fifties nightclub singer **Nichelle "Uhura" Nichols** recorded several albums, each more spacey than the last, the wildest one being *Out Of This World* (GNP Crescendo, 1991). Her voice sounds fine, but occasionally she'll disappear entirely on a low note, or shriek like Mrs. Miller on a high note. And the backup band, heavy on cheesy synthesizers, sounds like the house band at the Klingon Holiday Inn disco lounge. But fans will enjoy the bonus half-hour interview;

**Nichelle Nichols
Out Of This World
featuring "Gene"
GNP Records CD, 1991**

plus, all the songs have appropriately hokey space themes, such as "Beyond Antares" (which she sang on the TV show), a vocal version of the *Star Trek* theme, and "Gene," an ode to Gene Roddenberry which appears in both sung and recited versions. In the notes, the gushing lyrics about *Star Trek* creator Roddenberry's cosmic importance ("Gene, you always soar with eagles! Great bird of my galaxy!") are undermined by a snapshot of a bemused Roddenberry in his blue V-neck sweater, looking for all the galaxy like a suburban insurance man just back from the golf links. In 1976, Gene himself cut an obscure spoken LP with tracks such as "Star Trek Philosophy," and an instrumental version of the theme song. Alas, no singing! This proves he *was* the brains behind *Star Trek* after all.

Grace Lee Whitney
Disco Trekin'
Star Enterprise 45, 1976

If you chuckled at Nichelle's CD, then you will need a change of underwear after hearing **Grace Lee "Yeoman Janice Rand" Whitney's** 45, "Disco Trekin'" (Star Enterprise, 1976). It features a disco beat, wah-wah guitars, the jazzy refrain "Disco trekin' on a star!" and Whitney's loopy, stratospheric vocal swoops that sound like Minnie Ripperton on a roller coaster. George "Sulu" Takei revealed to us (after first asking, "Ooh, is *Shatner* in your book?!") that he sang the show stopping "Gong Song" on the Los Angeles cast LP of *Fly, Blackbird* in the early 1960s, but you may have to search the universe for more than five years to turn up a copy of that. Finally, we sadly report that DeForrest "Bones" Kelley never recorded ("Dammit, Jim, I'm an actor, not a singer!"). In his book, *Star Trek Movie Memories,* Shatner recalls that while filming *Star Trek V,* Kelley had to sing "Row, Row, Row Your Boat" and was so awful, he convulsed Shatner and Nimoy. We'd love to hear singing so bad, those two dare to laugh at it!

The singing virus that infected the Enterprise has now been passed on to the Next Generation. Witness **Brent "Data" Spiner's** CD, *Ol' Yellow Eyes Is Back* (Infinite Visions, 1991), with backup vocals by Jonathan Frakes Patrick Stewart, LeVar Burton, and Michael Dorn. Spiner grew up in a family of music lovers (the CD has a photo of him at sixteen with Judy Garland),

Brent Spiner
Ol' Yellow Eyes Is Back
Infinite Visions CD, 1991

appeared on Broadway in *Big River* and *Sunday In The Park With George,* and picked some real classics for this CD: Gershwin's "Embraceable You," William Frawley's "Carolina In The Mornin'," Regis Philbin's oldie "Toot-Toot-Tootsie, Goodbye," etc. Spiner's a pretty good light tenor, in a Broadway chorus boy kinda way; he sounds like Michael Feinstein or Mandy Patinkin with the vibrato knob turned up to eleven. Overall, his CD is technically superior to any of the old *Star Trek* actors' stuff: it's quite competently performed, tastefully restrained, well produced, and in no way at all embarrassing. But it's not very exciting, either. In other words, he's good, but he's no William Shatner!

Patty Duke
Don't Just Stand There
United Artists Records LP, 1965

Many of the records in this book could cause anguish for the listener, but only Patty Duke's records contributed to the mental breakdown of the performer. An incredibly gifted young actress, Duke was cursed with a horrific childhood. She reveals in her candid autobiography, *Call Me Anna*, that her dysfunctional parents simply handed her over to another couple who acted as her surrogate parents/managers. They changed her name and treated her as a cash cow, driving her to phenomenal success (Broadway stardom at thirteen in *The Miracle Worker*, an Oscar at sixteen), but starved her for love and attention, and completely overlooked her tendencies to manic depression.

Although she hated taking the voice lessons her mentors forced on her (she was grossed out by her teacher, who ate banana and cream cheese sandwiches on raisin bread with buttermilk while Patty was practicing scales), she did enjoy singing. That is, she enjoyed it until her handlers shoved her into the recording studio to cash in on the success of *The Patty Duke Show* (1963- 66). She was forced to stand in front of an orchestra and try to sing, even though her tiny voice was hardly musical. Because she couldn't read music, the producer had to tap her on the shoulder when it was time for her to begin. She did endless takes to get enough good pieces to paste together one usable version, and the stress and humiliation often made her break down sobbing. She later said that every song she recorded was "a painful extraction from my psyche."

We wish we could say that all that suffering translated into great art. To be kind, let's just say that these albums sound like what you'd get if you recorded an ordinary teenage girl of 1965, singing along to the radio in her bedroom. Patty's anorexically thin voice is bolstered by more overdubs than anyone since Annette Funicello (or maybe that's just Cousin Cathy joining in), but all to no avail: it just sounds like a whole lot of bad singers singing at once. The songs are a mixture of lackluster originals and wimpy covers: "What The World Needs Now," "Downtown," "Danke Schoen" (she sounds remarkably like Wayne Newton on a bad day), and "World Without Love" (her fans didn't know how appropriate the line "Please, lock me away!" really was). She recorded other albums, all virtually identical; her second, *Patty*, features a cover of the Beatles' "Yesterday" that may not be the worst of the 2,500+ covers of this song, but it's definitely in the bottom five. But we chose this one because it features her only big hit, the turgid "Don't Just Stand There," which hit number eight on the *Billboard* charts. (That's as hard to believe as "identical cousins"!). These days, Ms. Duke calls her albums "awful," and says that just seeing the ugly covers gives her stomach pains. If you must ask her to autograph one, please don't do it in a restaurant, because they kill her appetite. Trust us, we know the feeling.

Dwayne Hickman
"School Dance"
ABC Paramount Records 45, 1958

In his amusing autobiography, *Forever Dobie,* Dwayne Hickman recalls that in 1958 he was playing nephew Chuck on *The Bob Cummings Show* (aka *Love That Bob*) when the producers came up with the bright idea of making him a singing idol. Hickman quickly began taking voice lessons twice a week, while the higher ups carefully selected his debut song (an irritating tune called "School Dance" that sounds a bit like the horrid "Let's Dance" by Chris Montez). Soon, Hickman was on his reluctant way to a humiliating but short-lived (about one week) career as a singing sensation.

At the studio, the musicians didn't bother to hide their contempt for the nervous young incompetent. To make matters worse, Frank Sinatra was recording next door, and Steve Lawrence dropped by to watch the neophyte perform! After many aborted takes, producer Don Costa finally just recorded the backing track and dismissed the musicians. Hickman then sang along with the tape until they got enough takes (about thirty!) to patch together one acceptable version, which still sounds like a bad Ricky Nelson impersonator. Even Hickman himself has accurately described his singing voice as being alternately flat or sharp, or off-key, or one beat ahead of the music, or two beats behind. In a futile attempt to distract the listener, the backup singers simply shout "School dance!" at random moments in an obnoxious, adenoidal sneer, like a bad road company of *Grease.*

Next, it was time to promote this Frankenstein monster. ABC Paramount Records booked Hickman on *American Bandstand,* where he was forced to follow Frankie Avalon, and his lip-synching fell far behind the record, much to the bafflement of the hostile audience. Toweling off the flop sweat, he embarked on a tour of radio stations, but the only DJs who would talk to him were deep-night plattermen at tiny stations who were desperate for company. The final stop was the New York office of label president Sam Clark. Clark called in Paul Anka, who at that time was seventeen and had scored four consecutive Top 20 hits. Anka listened to eight bars of "School Dance," shook his head ruefully, then walked out without a word. Hickman was sent home, and plans to turn him into a singer were wisely scrapped. At least, he took it philosophically: he told himself that it didn't matter if he couldn't sing, because he had a talent for acting, and that's something that Frankie Avalon could certainly never say!

Two years later, when Hickman was starring as *Dobie Gillis,* Capitol somehow convinced him to record an album, *Dobie!* But his singing had not improved, and *Dobie!* sank like a bronze statue of "The Thinker." There's a great story attached to that record, too, but we'll save it for *More Hollywood Hi-Fi.* As for Hickman, he eventually became a CBS executive, perhaps so he could boss around tone-deaf teenage TV stars for a change!

Edd Byrnes
Kookie
Star of "77 Sunset Strip"
Warner Bros. Records LP, 1959

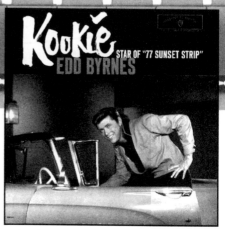

Trying to explain the Edd "Kookie" Byrnes craze of '59 to modern kids is like trying to explain a seventeenth-century Chinese opera libretto to a tadpole. Some things just belong to a certain time and place and do not travel well. Suffice it to say that Kookie was sort of a Fonzie or Fresh Prince of the late 1950s: a super-cool guy who got laughs on ABC's *77 Sunset Strip* by playing off the squares around him. His L-7 pals were Efrem Zimbalist, Jr., and Roger (Mr. Ann-Margret) Smith, the well-tailored detectives whose office was next door to Dino's, the restaurant where Kookie parked cars.

Kookie's trademarks were his elaborately Brylcreemed pompadour, which he was constantly combing, and his "Kookie-isms," a relentless stream of hipster jargon that made *High School Confidential* sound like Shakespeare. For example: "Dig it, Daddy-O, it's been a dark seven [a rough week]. I was piling up the Z's [sleeping] when I had to crack my peepers [wake up] to play like a pigeon [deliver a message] for a chickie who had the vital statistics at *all* the altitudes [she was stacked]..." This inane jive-talk bit made Byrnes a sensation, and he was quick to cash in. First came the hit single, "Kookie, Kookie (Lend Me Your Comb)," in which Connie Stevens begged to use Kookie's precious comb (why not borrow his handkerchief? It would be more sanitary!), while he fended her off with a barrage of impenetrable gibberish. It's on this LP, along with eleven other "ginchy" new songs, all basically the same: the band plays faux jazz or rock 'n' roll, while Kookie just talks his patented line of baffling beatnik B.S.

The titles tell you all you need to know: "The Kookie Cha Cha Cha," "Like, I Love You," and "Square Dance For Round Cats." Joanie Summers pops up on "Hot Rod Rock," and Byrnes actually sings a couple of lines with her. He sounds a bit like Fabian, and that's not a compliment. And Cole Porter fans will most assuredly "dig" "You're The Top," in which Porter's elegant English becomes "He's a nowhere drip who isn't hip to bop." Oh, well, it's better than what Cybill Shepherd did to him.

The year 1959 also brought a Kookie Christmas single ("Yulesville") and a 45 called "Kookie's Love Song." The B side was a special mix without Joanie Summers, so you could pretend *you* were talking with Kookie! Or, you could take the same money and buy yourself a life. A *77 Sunset Strip* soundtrack LP was a huge hit, too, although solo records by Smith and Zimbalist stiffed. Byrnes walked off the show, unwisely demanding more screen time, and his Kookie character miraculously leaped from parking lot attendant to detective (was this affirmative action for the tragically hip?). With so much exposure, his audience quickly tired of him. In 1963, in a supreme irony, Kookie was fired by the show's new producer, the squarest man in the world, Jack Webb! Like, "Ouchville!"

Arch Hall, Jr.
"Valerie" b/w "Vickie"
Spectra Records 45, 1962

True bad movie buffs will instantly recognize Arch Hall, Jr., as winner of the Tori Spelling Lifetime Achievement Award for Nepotism. Despite having almost zero acting ability, he starred in a half dozen movies. Despite his minimal singing talent and a mastery of about two and a half guitar chords, he sang in most of those movies, and cut records of his feeble warblings. Why? Perhaps it's because the president and top producer, director and screenwriter of Fairway International Productions, which kept casting Arch Hall, Jr., were all named... Arch Hall, Sr.

Both "Vickie" and its virtually identical flip side, "Valerie" (*not* the Monkees song "Valleri") come from Master Hall's second movie, *Eegah!* (1962), which marked the screen debut of the giant actor Richard "Jaws" Kiel. This $15,000 drive-in cheapie, about a huge caveman menacing some teenage airheads, went on to gross over a million dollars worldwide, but we doubt that any of that came from soundtrack sales. Both songs are deathly slow ballads, with tunes so basic they sound like beginning guitar finger exercises. Both feature female backup singers cooing, "Oohooh-waaaah!" in voices so high, they must've used a dog whistle for a pitch pipe. And both boast the sixteen-year-old prince of bland mediocrity, Arch Hall, Jr., who wheezes and whines so anemically, it sounds like someone punched him in the stomach just before the recording session began. (They should've waited until after the session, when they had a good reason.) "Valerie" starts with a slow whistling solo, and the guy can't even whistle on key. But we do give him credit as a songwriter for having the guts to rhyme "Valerie" with "salary" and "calorie."

Hall Senior only cast Hall Junior because he had tiny budgets, and his son would work for peanuts. But debate still rages over whether Hall the Younger actually had any talent. (Hall himself didn't seem to think so: he quit movies in 1965, served heroically in Vietnam, then became an airline pilot.) There is now a thriving cult that claims his performances have merit beyond their camp value. In his book, *Hollywood Rock,* singer/songwriter Marshall Crenshaw gave *Eegah!* four stars and said Hall is "in fine form." The Medved brothers named it one of the "50 Worst Films Of All Time" and called Hall "tone-deaf." Leonard Maltin wrote that Hall's *Wild Guitar* (1962) is a "perfectly awful melodrama," while Crenshaw gave it five stars (perhaps because it, too, features the immortal "Vickie"), and said, "I think it's better than *Gone With The Wind!*" Perhaps, as Hall's cult insists, it's time for a reappraisal. Well, you can pop *Eegah!* or *Wild Guitar* or *The Nasty Rabbit* (1964) into the VCR if you want, but we've sat through these turkeys enough times already. We think we'll just pay one of our teenage relatives to watch them again *for* us.

Raquel Welch
"I'm Ready To Groove"
A Swingin' Summer Soundtrack
H.B.R. Records LP, 1965

The young Raquel Welch had two huge talents, and she showed them both in her first featured movie role. We mean, of course, she was both an amusingly bad actress and a rib-ticklingly lousy singer.

In 1965, with the "beach movie" genre in full swing, United Screen Arts released *A Swingin' Summer,* a mindless teen romp with a twist: it was set not at the beach, but in a scenic mountain resort at Lake Arrowhead, California (which later burned down, no doubt torched by movie lovers). The almost nonexistent plot was merely an excuse for lots of songs by such teen dreamboats as the Righteous Brothers, Donnie "Mr. Personality" Brooks, Gary Lewis & The Playboys, and The Rip Chords. Just to keep the guys awake, the movie also introduced "TV's Hollywood Palace Billboard Girl, Raquel Welch" (actually, she had bit parts in two previous films, including *Roustabout* in 1964, but appearing in an Elvis movie apparently doesn't qualify as an "acting debut"). Plausibly enough, Raquel plays a repressed bookworm who spends much of the film clad in naught but black horn-rim glasses and an itsy bitsy teenie weenie white bikini that struggles to contain her built-in book shelf.

At last comes the scene all B-movie fans were waiting for: Raquel yanks off her glasses, shakes out her hair bun, and, Gasp! Why, she's be-yoo-tiful! She announces her sexual liberation by singing "I'm Ready To Groove," a "hot mama" blues shouter in the "I'm a W-O-M-A-N" mold, with lyrics about how much better it is for a girl to have a boyfriend than to be literate ("I usta dig Freud! And Shakespeare, too! But no more, baby! 'Cuz I dig yooooooou!"). While Raquel made the horny wolves in the movie howl, her take on Howlin' Wolf just made moviegoers howl with laughter. Her Chipmunky yipping sounds like George Thorogood singing "Bad To The Bone" after sucking down two tanks of helium. The movie makers, no fools they, plastered the soundtrack LP with photos of Raquel in her white bikini, along with smirking liner notes lauding the imposing talents of "the bountifully endowed Miss Welch." We half expected to find a sticker saying, "No echo chambers were necessary in the recording of this track."

Over the past thirty years, Raquel has done an admirable job of fighting gravity. We are happy to report that the only thing on her that got lower was her voice, which is now about an octave deeper and much more pleasant. After suffering twenty years of being bludgeoned by critics, Raquel's mature singing voice finally earned her some good notices, both in Las Vegas and on Broadway in *Woman of the Year,* although it's possible her voice seemed better than it really was, since she took over her Broadway role from fellow musically challenged sexpot Lauren Bacall.

Farrah Fawcett
"You"
Nelson Barry Records 45, 1978

In 1978, Elvis Costello sang, "You see her picture in a thousand places, 'cause she's This Year's Girl," and everyone just knew he was referring to Farrah Fawcett. With her bright Pepsodent smile and blond lion's mane, Farrah revolutionized the concept of the pinup girl by combining sunny wholesomeness with blatant sexuality. Her top-rated ABC series, *Charlie's Angels,* gave us the term "jiggle show," and a poster of her in a red swimsuit became the most popular dorm wallpaper in history, selling over eight million copies (possibly because she was the first TV star to display such prominent nipple bumps since *Batman*'s Adam West). The torrent of Farrah-phernalia also included dolls, wigs, a quickie biography, and this 45, a re-release of a flop single cut in her pre-Angel days. At least, she had the good taste to nix a scheme to sell bottled water from her kitchen faucet, although "Farrah's Fawcett Water" probably would've been more popular than this record, and not half as drippy.

"You" is the type of overwrought French ballad that you hear playing behind love scenes in those sleazy European sex movies that Showtime burns off after midnight. Jean-Paul Vignon does the actual singing in French (and the way he puffs and howls, it must've been pretty hard work), while Farrah provides running commentary in the form of overdubbed, whispered pillow talk (*see "Rock Hudson"*). The trouble with this idea is that all of Farrah's sex appeal resides in her physical appearance. Take away the cascades of hair, the enticing overbite, the nipple bumps, etc., and Farrah is no more capable of conveying sexual passion with her voice alone than was Jack Webb. She sounds like a ten-year-old girl reading from the Kama Sutra in a stage whisper, with absolutely no idea what she's talking about. When she describes a moonlit walk with her lover by whispering, "I could hear the grass bend under our feet," you don't get turned on, you just marvel at how well she could hear with all that hair over her ears. And when Farrah really gets carried away with sexual abandon, whispering, "You! You! You!" over and over, her Texas twang makes the word come out as "Ee-yew! Ee-yew! Ee-yew!" Sounds like she stepped into something unpleasant when she was walking in that noisy grass!

This was one of the few Farrah Fawcett items that was not a hot seller, perhaps because of the disappointing lack of nipple bumps on the picture sleeve. Farrah never made another record (not even the obvious duet with Whisperin' Bill Anderson), but she did finally manage to leave her seventies sexpot image behind and earn respect as an actress, while her old hairdo still survives on the heads of countless Oklahoma mall rats. These days, when the oldies station plays "This Year's Girl," you just know Elvis is referring to Cindy Crawford, or maybe Tyra Banks...certainly not Farrah Fawcett! We would bet that no one is more relieved about that than Farrah.

Jayne Mansfield
"That Makes It!"
Original Sound Records 45, 1964

Back in the 1950s, every Hollywood studio needed a buxom, bleached blond Marilyn Monroe look-alike, and the top contenders were Jayne Mansfield and Mamie Van Doren. Sharing only two of Marilyn's assets (and we certainly don't mean talent or charisma), these top heavy bombshells managed to be eye-popping window dressing in a number of low-budget time wasters and even made a couple of cult classics: *The Girl Can't Help It* (Jayne, 1956) and *High School Confidential* (Mamie, 1958). But by 1963, Jayne's and Mamie's fortunes were sagging. Marilyn was dead, and the popularity of the boyish Audrey Hepburn had deflated the vogue for protruding peroxide princesses. So why not try new careers as rock 'n' roll singers!

On "That Makes It," Jayne, the poor man's Marilyn Monroe, proves that having a forty-inch chest doesn't necessarily give you enough lung power to be a singer. "That Makes It" is a lame and rather late answer record to the 1958 classic "Chantilly Lace," in which we hear what was on the other end of that famous telephone conversation. Naturally, it starts with a phone ringing. It must be the long-deceased Big Bopper calling *very* long distance, because Jayne (The Big Topper?) picks it up, and in a breathy voice that might be sexy if she weren't putting the emphasis on all the wrong syllables, says, "HellOOOOO?...Yes, THIS is Jayne, bay-BEE... You want WHAT?... A girl like MEEEE?" Is she running a phone sex service for dead people? The music now kicks in (it sounds like a burlesque-house pit band playing "Chantilly Lace," with a few notes changed), and Jayne begins cooing about what kind of man she wants. To wit: "With LONG, black hair, he can't BE no square! 'Cause when he kisses my LIPS, he's gotta MAKE me flip!... Ooh, baby! That MAKES it!" Sure, it's dumb, but it shows why Jayne was so well cast as a no-talent rock singer whose voice shatters glass in *The Girl Can't Help It*.

This rare gem, along with its flip side, a heavy-breathing rendition of "Little Things Mean A Lot" (as if Jayne had *anything* that was little) can now be found on an elaborate CD compilation, *Too Hot To Handle* (Legend). It also includes live appearances, interviews, movie and TV soundtrack clips, and both sides of a weird 1965 U.K. single, "As The Clouds Drift By" (a vaguely psychedelic pop tune combines with Jayne's atonal, baby-talk vocal to create what sounds like the great, lost Patty Duke record) b/w "Suey" (the band vamps, and Jayne steps to the mike at random moments to squeal something provocative yet inexplicable, like, "Ooh! It makes my liver quiver!"). The desultory guitar twanging on these two cuts is rumored to be provided by slumming session cat Jimi Hendrix. This was probably the gig that made him decide to start taking drugs.

Mamie Van Doren and June Wilkinson
"Bikini With No Top On The Top"
Jubilee Records 45, 1963

Mamie Van Doren was much more musical than Jayne, having been a club singer and wife of big band leader Ray Anthony. According to her autobiography, *Playing The Field,* she stOOd out from the crowd in 1950s Hollywood by embracing rock 'n' roll, both musically (she sang rock tunes in her own grade-Z films and cooed "The Girl Who Invented Rock 'n Roll" to Clark Gable in her lone prestige picture, *Teacher's Pet)* and literally, thanks to her close relationships with Elvis Presley and Eddie Cochran. She wasn't a great rock singer, but she was way out in front of Jayne Mansfield (but then, Jayne was way out in front of herself, too).

However, for 1963's sublimely grating "Bikini With No Top On The Top," all attempts at singing went straight out the window. Mamie was joined on this record by June "The Bosom" Wilkinson (the poor man's Mamie Van Doren, if you can imagine such a thing) and a third, uncredited glamour girl from Mamie and June's then-current potboiler, *The Candidate.* This titillating trio simply chanted the song in the kind of "brassy-broad" growls you would expect from a gaggle of strippers, which is appropriate, since it is all about how they became famous by exposing their whopping mammaries. It seems that one day, they went to the beach for some innocent topless sunbathing, and imagine their surprise when they were mobbed by men! ("Eyes would pop! Call a cop! Bikini with no top on the top!" they honk, over a blaring saxophone, and you can practically hear their gum snapping.) They are arrested, but parlay their notoriety into a layout for *Playboy.* ("Hey, pop! Flip your mop! Bikini with no top on the top!") And now, they're movie stars, all because they took off their tops (Flop! Flop!) Mamie claims the producer talked them into doffing their bullet bras and recording topless, which explains why the band sounds so sloppy and distracted. This record gives new meaning to the phrase, "You really had to be there."

Jayne and Mamie never recorded together, but they did costar in the 1966 bomberoo, *Las Vegas Hillbillies,* with the great male sex symbol, Ferlin Husky. Mamie denied rumors that she and Jayne fought constantly, explaining that they couldn't have, because they refused to be in the same room together. Of course, it's possible there just wasn't a room big enough to hold both of them at the same time.

If you would like to hear even more nonmelodious singing by amply-endowed, B-movie sex goddesses, pick up Rhino Records' compilation album *Va-Va-Voom!* Or any Madonna record.

Brigitte Bardot
"Harley Davidson"
A3 Records 45, 1968

...And God
Created
The Woman...

It is difficult to overstate the impact of Brigitte Bardot on American culture. Beginning with her first big movie, *And God Created Woman* (1956), BB's fresh, open sexuality and willingness to shed her clothing not only attracted millions of moviegoers who thought they'd never sit through a subtitled "art film" but also fired the first shots in the coming sexual revolution, marking the beginning of the end for the tightly laced Eisenhower years.

Less well known is the French sex kitten's huge contribution to pop music. BB cut a number of records during the sixties and early seventies, several of which were big hits in France. She loved to sing, even though she didn't have much of a voice (after recording several hits, she got serious and began taking voice lessons, a course of action we recommend to fellow sex kitten Madonna). She mostly talk-sang the uptempo tunes, and whispered the ballads in a voice that sounded like a much, much sexier Hervé Villechaize. But of course, her singing wasn't why anyone bought these records, and that's where her contribution to music comes in. BB sang in a series of worldwide New Year's TV specials, the most important of which aired in 1968. The music was nothing to get excited over: a typical cut is "Harley-Davidson," a peppy but tuneless Europop ditty for which BB chants the lyrics in French (we think it's about a motorcycle or something). What mattered about this special is that BB prerecorded her seventeen songs, then lip-synched them as she was filmed frolicking in various exotic locales. These mini-films had storylines built around the lyrics, and naturally, all showed off the delectable face and form of la fair BB (the "Harley" clip was "Lady Godiva On A Motorbike"). Get it now? This was the first-ever television broadcast of glamorous, dramatized, lip-synched pop music clips featuring a half-naked sex kitten! That's right, kids: Brigitte Bardot invented MTV!

Also in 1968, Brigitte and her "close friend," singer/songwriter Serge Gainsbourg, recorded the infamous "Je T'aime... Moi Non Plus," a song that featured lots of heavy breathing and simulated sex over an instrumental track. Her furious husband, Gunther Sachs, demanded that it not be released, so Gainsbourg obligingly locked the tape away. Two years later, he recut the song with another consenting adult, his wife, Jane Birkin, and it became an international sensation, the "Love To Love You Baby" of its time. Too bad BB's version wasn't released in '68; it seems appropriate that she be the one to introduce aural sex to America. Today, BB devotes her time to animal rights, and hasn't made a record in years. But her old songs still sell like hot cakes in Europe, where many have been released as picture discs, featuring the young, kittenish BB sans clothing. *Vive la France!*

Fabio
After Dark
Scotti Brothers CD, 1993

We're told that Fabio's record contract forbids the reproduction of his CD cover unless the reviewer is saying something positive about it. So you won't see it here... nor anywhere else, we'd wager.

You no longer have to be a woman to be a siren (or to sing like one). Civilization has advanced to the point where men, too, can at last achieve fame and fortune as bleached-blond bimbos! And so, we devote a place here to that bewilderingly popular romance novel cover boy, Fabio. Besides, he belongs here, because his chest is bigger than Jayne Mansfield's.

Aside from four words on "When Somebody Loves Somebody," Fabio does not sing on this CD. Instead, he pontificates on what is "romahnteek," á la Jack Webb, only in a thick, oily Italian accent that makes Steve Martin and Dan Aykroyd's "wild an' crazy" swingers, the Festrunk brothers, sound like Cary Grant. All of Fabio's ruminations on "luuuuhv" are accompanied by the type of sleazy Eurotrash disco-jazz that is normally heard behind sex scenes on the Playboy Channel. And what are Fabio's mystical secrets of amour? As it turns out, they are distressingly pedestrian: send her flowers, take her out to dinner, visit a tropical island, and take a "wok on da bitch" (we hoped he was about to reveal some ancient sex trick involving Chinese food, but it turned out he was just trying to say "walk on the beach"). In short, every personal ad cliché in the book. Is this *all* Fabio knows about romance?! Well, at one point, he oozes that he likes to surprise his special lady "weeth a plahn teeket, her toosbrush, an' her bahkeenee." We're sure the sight of him in her bikini surprised her, but what was he doing with her toothbrush?! ("That's okay, Fabio! You can keep it!")

This CD alternates Fabio's malapropian make-out lessons with mood music by Billy Ocean, Dionne Warwick, and other Adult Contemporary mainstays. (Fabio's Romance Cliché number 9: "Poot on a *sexy* rahdio stahshun!") In an ill-conceived programming decision, the last song is by the master of sex talk, Barry White. Barry's post-orgasmic rumble only serves to remind us of how wimpy Fabio sounds, and how little he seems to know about romance in comparison. In fact, the only feeling this CD left us with was depression at the very thought that there might be women lonely and pathetic enough to sit around listening to such drivel and gazing at the photos of this preening Adonis. This ludicrous CD conjures up the image of a man who apparently views all women as interchangeable ninnies who react identically to the same dumb timeworn lines and gestures, sort of like Anthony Quinn with Farrah Fawcett's hairdo. Oh sure, he calls the one he's with at the moment "mah spahshul laydee," but that's probably just because he can't recall her name offhand. We suggest that romance fans skip this album and instead pick up the truly romantic *Album Of Love Songs* (State Etat, 1978, U.K.) by Dame Barbara Cartland, which at least answers the musical question "What would Mrs. Miller sound like with a British accent?" We're reserving a "vurry spahshul" place for this laydee in our next book.

Steve Allen
How's Your Sister?
Dot Records 45, 1964

Noel Coward once called Steve Allen "the most talented man in America," and it's easy to see why. Allen is a fine pianist, composer of over 5,200 songs, author of books on every topic from comedy to the Bible, and inventor of almost everything about talk shows that's worth taking credit for (such as dumping the host into a vat of Jell-O, which we'd like to see Geraldo try... and hold him under for a while). But to us, Steve Allen's greatest achievement is this record, the immortal "How's Your Sister?"

When we approached Allen for information on this obscure gem, he was amazingly gracious, but between the lines, we thought we detected a hint of dismay. Perhaps he thought, "All the stuff I've done, and you dopes want to write about "How's Your Sister?" He sent us so much information (including twenty one cassettes full of his songs! Thanks!), we suspect he was secretly hoping we'd realize how insignificant it was and forget all about it. But how could we possibly forget a record that set two of the silliest catchphrases of all time to a tune you could really twist to?!

All seriousness aside, Allen recalls that this song, written for his TV show, came from his discovery that he could always get an inexplicable laugh just by asking someone, "How's your sister?" He also got laughs by reciting the inane lyrics of current rock hits as if they were poetry. Combining these ideas, he wrote a rock 'n' roll song for which his catchphrases provided the meaningless lyrics. Not even Sebastian Cabot could read these lines out loud with a straight face: "Well, hi there, Mister! How's your sister? Does she still go, 'Schmock! Schmock!'?" (for full effect, "Schmock! Schmock!" must be delivered in a high-pitched shriek, like a cockatoo getting his tail pulled). Allen also works such favorite words as "schtick," "yick," "creel," "clyde," "fink," and "slauson" into the song, before ending on a huge crescendo: "Does she!... Still go!... SCHMOCK! SCHMOOOOOOOOOOOOOOOOOOCK!!!!!" Man, that'll clear your sinuses! Maybe Dylan should cover it.

Allen puts this into what he calls the "goof-ola" category, or songs that are silly but not clever. To demonstrate the difference, he sent us a tape titled "Flop Sweat," containing more recent comedy songs ("Blamin' The Jews," a Hawaiian song called "Three Mile Island," etc.), which are funny, but in a more cerebral, Mark Russell fashion. Allen is a brilliant man, but we hope he's not embarrassed to be associated with this great 45, a slice of pure idiot humor that is the musical equivalent of that photo of Einstein sticking his tongue out. This type of nonsense defies intellectual analysis, but so what? Every so often, in this high pressure world, you just need to take a moment to yourself, throw back your head, and scream, "Schmock! Schmock!"

Jack Paar
"Funny What You Learn From Women" b/w "Blue Wiggle"
RCA Records 45, 1958

JACK PAAR RCA VICTOR 47-7306

FUNNY WHAT YOU LEARN FROM WOMEN and **BLUE WIGGLE**

This is one of the oddest records we've ever come across, but that's not surprising, seeing as how it's by a man whose major talent was unpredictability. Jack Paar hosted NBC's *Tonight Show* from 1957 to 1962; since then, aside from a short-lived attempt to compete with Carson on ABC, he has mostly avoided the limelight. Consequently, his fame has grown dimmer with each passing year. But during his five-year heyday, Paar was one of the most talked about figures in America, simply because nobody knew *what* he might say or do next.

Unlike previous *Tonight Show* hosts (Steve Allen, Ernie Kovacs), Paar was not a skilled entertainer. He had enjoyed minor success as a stand-up comic, but mostly worked for CBS as a chat show host and game show emcee (he once joked that he had no talent, but was too big a star to quit show business, and he named a Ramrod compilation LP of his *Tonight Show* material *The Best of What's His Name).* What made him so fascinating to watch was the fact that he did *not* put up a smooth, professional veneer, but instead wore all his emotions and neuroses right on the surface, for the whole world to see. He feuded openly with other celebrities, asked questions that offended guests, lauded Fidel Castro's revolutionary forces in Cuba, and once stormed off the show in tears when the NBC censors cut a "water closet" joke from his monologue. Paar's volatile personality turned a cozy talk show into a riveting nightly psycho-drama: It was like staring at a ticking time bomb and wondering when, or if, it would go off.

This weird 45 elicits that same antsy feeling of anticipation. Both sides are simply vamps played by a small rock group and built around a hypnotic, repeating bass line, topped with eerie, theremin-like whistling by songwriter Jerry Teifer. Every eight bars or so, Paar steps to the microphone and speaks a few words, in a slow-as-molasses voice that must have inspired Steve Martin's "Luuuuv Gaaaaahd" character. On "Funny What You Learn From Women," the band vamps while Paar ruminates on what women teach you...(vamp)... "'bout fallin' in love"...(vamp, vamp)... "'bout kissin'"...(vamp, whistle)...and so on for a good two minutes. Finally, the punch line arrives: "But the one I'll never forget is Belinda"...(vamp, whistle, vamp)... "She taught me...to *whistle*..." "Blue Wiggle" is even weirder: Paar kicks it off with "Didja ever see a... *blue wiggle*?"...(vamp)... "Soooo blue"...(vamp)... "Baaaaby blue"... (vamp, whistle, vamp)... "Royal buuuuh-looooooooo"...(whistle, vamp, whistle)... "Blue, bluuuuue...WIG-gull!"...(vamp, whistle, fadeout). And that's it: no explosion, no tantrum, no nothin'! At least, not *this* time. But say, let's play it again! No telling what that crazy Jack Paar might do *next* time around!...

Joey Bishop
Sings Country & Western
ABC Records LP, 1968

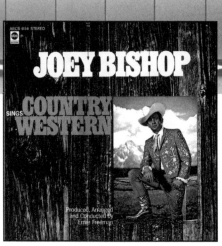

Deadpan comic and Vegas Rat Pack hanger-on Joey Bishop was one of the few reasonably successful challengers to Johnny Carson's late night throne, but his first few weeks on ABC did not bode well for the future. For his debut telecast in 1967, Bishop tried to counter Carson by booking Jack Paar, the former *Tonight Show* host, who immediately commandeered Joey's desk and began interviewing Ethel Merman and Juliet Prowse himself, while Joey was reduced to mumbling ineffectually from his own guest couch. Over on NBC that night, Carson welcomed Bob Hope, Sen. Robert Kennedy, and the Rev. Billy Graham, with a surprise walk-on appearance by Billy's pal, God. Carson pulled a staggering 48% share of the audience, while Bishop started with 12% and dropped to 4% by the time the show whimpered to a halt.

No wonder Joey began looking around for another line of work! "Country singer" seems an unusual career choice for a nice Jewish boy from the Bronx, but at that point, anything looked better than hosting a talk show, and it had to be easier to compete with Johnny Cash than with Johnny Carson. After all, Joey already had the monotone singing voice. All he had to do was round up a load of classic country tunes ("Born To Lose," "Cold, Cold Heart," etc.), get some "countrypolitan" orchestra-and-chorus arrangements (can't sound too hicky if you're gonna play Vegas), and of course, buy himself one of those hilarious rhinestone Nudie suits with matching spangly boots that guys like Porter Wagoner wore (we'll bet you 8 to 1 he didn't pay retail for the suit). The cover photo of this album alone is funnier than the first six weeks of *The Joey Bishop Show* put together.

As for the music itself: Joey not only can't sing, he hardly even tries. His whispery, tentative voice is barely there; at times, he is drowned out by his own backup singers. It's like listening to a Ray Price concert, except that Price's microphone has accidentally been set up at a dark corner table where a depressed, nebbishy accountant is drinking double martinis and singing along halfheartedly to the sad music to take his mind off the fact that his date didn't show up. Halfway through side two, Joey has abandoned any efforts to stay within twenty feet of the melody, and he ends "Your Cheatin' Heart" by bitterly grumbling, "Nobody likes a cheatin' chick!" There's one more cut to go, but we'll just tiptoe quietly away and leave Joey to nurse his drink and dream of asking his buddy Frank to arrange some revenge on that bitch who stood him up. By the way, the liner notes for this album include plaudits for Joey's country singing debut from no less than Glen Campbell and Dean Martin! Glen has since confessed to suffering a drug habit that warped his perceptions, so we'll let him off the hook. But just how much vino did Dino drink that day?!

Regis Philbin
It's Time For Regis!
Mercury Records LP, 1968

IT'S TIME FOR REGIS!
REGIS PHILBIN

On this LP, America's most irascible talk show cohost blesses his fans with a collection of ballads, Broadway show tunes, and vaudeville chestnuts that truly take the "easy" out of "easy listening."

It's not that the lovable hothead is such a terrible singer, although God knows, he's no Steve Allen. It's just that Regis's light tenor is *so* light, on some tracks it simply seems to waft out of the speakers and dissipate into thin air. If only he sang as he speaks; i.e., if only he shouted every third or so word: "The SMILE!... You were SMILING!!... You were SMILING THEN!!!" At least, the listener would be kept awake. But what truly makes this album such a laff-riot is not Regis's passably mediocre vocalizing, but the velvety thick coating of 1960s Las Vegas cheesiness that blankets everything on it, from the cover photo of Rege under the ABC theater marquee in his lounge-lizard blue tux, mike in one hand, the other hand caught in mid-fingersnap, to the whiter-than-Casper orchestra and chorus arrangements that make Mitch Miller's Singalong Gang sound like Kool & The Gang. If your conception of heaven is getting stuck in an elevator with Regis Philbin, then this album is the answer to your prayers. Here are just a few of the out-Regis highlights:

Rodgers & Hart's immortal "Where Or When," arranged mid-sixties Burt Bacharach style, with a cha-cha beat!..."Toot, Toot, Tootsie (Goodbye)," which ends with Regis shouting over the fadeout, "Sock it to 'em, Tootsie!"...and liner notes by Regis's then-boss, would-be country singer Joey Bishop, who reassures wary record buyers that "for a man his age, he sings great."

For those audiophiles who demand their Regis in glorious digital stereo, Mercury reissued this record on CD in 1994, but the vinyl version is still worth picking up for a dollar or so, if only to get the back cover photo of Regis, Joey, and Sammy Davis, Jr., together, all decked out in cool Nehru jackets. Rege's and Joey's are gray, whereas Sammy's is hot pink. Now, quickly: Who's the *genuine* Vegas hepcat in this picture?

True Regis Heads will also want to scout up a copy of *Christmas Time*, (1988), Regis's private label Christmas album which, like all the finest Ronco Xmas gifts, was sold through TV only. And, of course, no Regis collection is complete without the yin to Regis's yang, Kathie Lee Gifford. America's most anal-retentive mommy has released a scary CD of lullabies, *Dreamship* (Warner Kids, 1996), plus a couple of gushy albums (both two-record sets!) on the Heartland label, *Sentimental Journey* (1992) and *Christmas With Kathie Lee* (1993). The first record sounds like Mary Poppins with a press agent, the second LP will give you a pretty good idea of what the Miss America talent competition must've sounded like during the big band era, and the third lets you hear what it would sound like if the pageant were held in December.

Johnny Carson, Ed McMahon, and Doc Severinsen

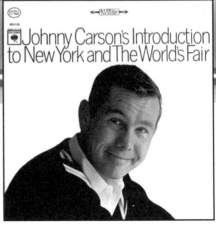

Johnny Carson's Introduction to New York and The World's Fair

No matter what your economic class, nodding off during *The Tonight Show* used to be one of the few things that every American shared. But then the abdication of King Johnny sparked the Late Night Wars, leaving insomniacs to channel surf forever among the feuding fiefdoms of Jay, Dave, and all the other chatty pretenders to the throne. Fortunately, you can still relive some of that old magic, thanks to a handful of obscure records.

Johnny Carson occasionally sang a few bars on the show (most famous was his impromptu duet with Bette Midler, captured on the "Best Of Carson" videos), but his few records are spoken word. The oddest is *Introduction To New York and The World's Fair,* an audio tour recorded in 1964 when Carson was still a fresh face on *The Tonight Show.* Best known is *Here's Johnny* (Casablanca, 1978), an LP of audio clips from *Tonight.* It's fun, but the videos are better, because you don't have to *imagine* the humorous sight of a hurled tomahawk sinking into a target's crotch.

In a perfect example of Hollywood logic, Carson never sang on record, while the famously untalented Ed McMahon cut both an album and a single. His album, *And Me...I'm Ed McMahon* (Cameo / Parkway, 1965), contained Hank Kingsley-esque renditions of such standards as "My Funny Valentine," "They Call The Wind Maria" (why not a trio with Clint Eastwood and Lee Marvin?), and "Try To Remember" (a phrase he probably heard a lot on the mornings after his famous nights out with Mr. Budweiser). But we prefer his 1971 Capitol 45, "Those Beautiful Girls" b/w "The God-Why-Don't-You-Love-Me Blues." Both are from Stephen Sondheim's *Follies* and deal with the pursuit of beautiful women (something Ed knows about firsthand), but it's the B-side that is Ed's best moment on vinyl. A patter song slowed to half-speed, it is ostensibly about fear of commitment, but with his tuneless vocalizing, Big Ed turns it into an anthem for every unappreciated, talent-deficient side-kick in television history. You can practically hear him crying, "God, why don't you love me as much as Carson?!" as he wearily schlepps off to host his ten-thousandth episode of *Star Search's Funniest Celebrity Bloopers.*

Doc Severinsen made many fine instrumental LPs, but we bet you've never heard "Oh, Mr. Dillon" (Epic, 1959), a 45 released ten years before he became Johnny's bandleader. It's a silly western novelty, featuring Doc's near perfect impression of Dennis "Chester" Weaver on *Gunsmoke.* In a twist on *High Noon,* Chester warns Marshal Dillon that a bad outlaw is a-gunnin' for him ("Oh, Mr. Dillon! There's been a killin'!" he honks through his nose). But Marshal Dillon heads the other way, using Chester as a shield! It sounds like the times during "Stump The Band" when Doc would ad-lib a goofy   hill-billy tune. Play it back-to-back with Johnny and Ed's records, and soon you'll once again be happily shouting "Hi-yo!" and falling asleep like a baby!

Arsenio Hall (Chunky A)
Large And In Charge
MCA Records CD, 1989

Like many a revolutionary, Arsenio Hall created a movement that eventually swept him aside. As the first African-American to host a national TV talk show, he was the first serious threat to Johnny Carson, and the first host to book rap stars who would never have gotten past Security at the old *Tonight Show*. And his raucous "house party" format became the model for all talk shows of the nineties (although it was painful to watch Dennis Miller doing obscure literary references for an audience of woofing meatheads who thought Kierkegaard was an imported beer). Unfortunately, by proving there was a big audience for hip, late night chat, Hall spawned a flood of imitators. In 1993, many stations bumped his show to make way for Chevy Chase's Fox Network atrocity, and Arsenio called it quits. (If only he'd waited six weeks!)

But back in November of 1989, Arsenio was red hot. That month alone, he made the cover of *Time* and released his first CD, *Large And In Charge,* as "Chunky A," a character he played on TV. Sporting huge shades, miles of gold chains, and an outrageously padded rear end, Chunky A was a parody of such well-fed rappers as the Fat Boys. Arsenio took the music seriously, enlisting producer A. Z. Groove to lay down a solid funk beat and lots of state-of-the-art hip-hop effects, while his lyrics poked fun at every rap and R&B cliché in the book. The title cut is a typical rapper's boast, only with cockeyed claims like "I got more moves than Ex-Lax!" The rapper fetish for big butts turns up in "Stank Breath," where Chunky falls for a girl with "a classic brick gluteus" (or "big ghetto booty, for those of you who're new to this"). But he "just can't do her," 'cause "her mouth smells like a sewer." "The Ho Is Lazy" lifts its chorus from Fine Young Cannibals' "She Drives Me Crazy," as Chunky disses his woman for watching soap operas all day, while she comes back at him ("Hey, Shamu! You call rappin' a *job*?!") like Aunt Esther ripping into Fred Sanford (Hall does both voices). Prince gets a much-deserved lampooning on the squeaky "Very High Key," while "Sorry" is a cool parody of a Boyz II Men-style R&B ballad. As the backup singers smoothly coo, "Sor-reee," Chunky blubbers apologies to his girl for all the little things he's done wrong: selling her car, putting her dog in the microwave, giving her a phony name, etc. The CD closes with one serious cut, Hall's anti-drug rap, "Dope, The Big Lie." It even features a cameo by Ice-T, continuing the fine public service work he began on the *Mr. T* LP, back in 1984.

This album may disappoint rap purists (there's not one obscenity, racial epithet, or dead cop on it), but it's a heck of a lot more fun than any of the wimpy records made by Hall's buddy Eddie "Party All The Time" Murphy. If you must listen to a TV star rap, better you should party down with Chunky A than with David Faustino, Raven-Symone, or Jack Webb. Now, come on, Arsenio! Let's get BUSY!!!...on a sequel.

Paul Shaffer and Greg Evigan
Greg & Paul "A Year At The Top"
Casablanca Records LP, 1977

Rock 'n' roll has many mysteries: What did Jerry Lee Lewis want to tell Elvis when he showed up at Graceland with pistol in hand? What did John see in Yoko? If Dylan ever blew his nose, could he still sing? And what would the Archies have sounded like had they been invented during the Bee Gees' disco period?

Well, ponder that last one no more, for here is your answer! *A Year At The Top* is a soundtrack LP for a sitcom that we guarantee you never saw. It premiered on NBC on August 5, 1977, and was yanked on September 4. (We're amazed they had enough time to make an album.) The show's premise was that two young musicians from Boise move to Hollywood, and their agent turns out to be Satan's son (not that implausible). He offers them "a year at the top" in trade for their souls. They refuse, but he constantly tempts them with glimpses of what stardom would be like. This lame premise provided plenty of excuses for even lamer songs, performed by those off-the-rack teen idols, dreamy hunk Greg Evigan and his kooky, huggable l'il buddy, Paul Shaffer... that's right, the future "Coolest Man In Late Night TV!"

Just like the Monkees and the Archies, Greg & Paul suffered under the musical direction of bubblegum impresario Don Kirshner, but this LP is co-produced and arranged by Paul, so he must share the blame for the album virtually defining the term "wimp rock." The lyrics are third-hand romantic or nothin's-gonna-stop-us-now clichés lifted from a thousand other songs and wedded to punchless tunes that mostly sound like "Philadelphia Freedom" with all the kick-ass, rock 'n' roll abandon bled out of it. Every cut could be the theme from a failed seventies TV show (one of them *is*: "A Year at the Top"!). These guys shouldn't fear the devil: they have no soul to lose. And speaking of wimpy, the vocals are pitched higher than Olivia Newton-John's. Perhaps this has something to do with the sausage-casing-tight pants Greg sports in the hilarious cover photo (also, check out the open-neck disco shirts and Paul's wide white belt! If the show had been as funny as this photo, it would still be on the air today).

Paul learned from this debacle and returned to *Saturday Night Live* with a devastating impression of Don Kirshner. (He once introduced the Blues Brothers by saying that, thanks to him, they are "no longer an authentic blues act, but have managed to become a viable commercial product.") Greg went on to play second banana to a chimp on NBC's *B.J. And The Bear* in 1979 (did Letterman sell him the monkey?), did a spy show called *Masquerade* that lasted a few months on ABC in 1984, and starred with our hero, William Shatner, on the USA Network's *Tek Wars* in 1995 (canceled after eighteen episodes). Maybe he should have signed that pact with Satan. Could Hell be any worse than *B.J. And The Bear*?

Cliff Arquette
Charlie Weaver Sings For His People
Columbia Records LP, 1959

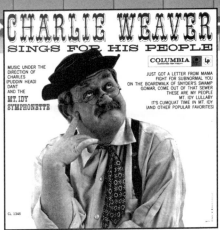

Today, Cliff Arquette is remembered mostly as a Hollywood Square and as the grandpa of Rosanna and Patricia Arquette. This is unfair, because he really did make a positive contribution to show business.

Born in 1905, Arquette began playing an elderly hick on radio, and just kept doing it until he didn't need makeup. Somewhere along the way, he named his character "Charlie Weaver," and the odd fictional image gradually blotted out his own identity. When TV arrived, he became a favorite guest star of Steve Allen, Jack Paar, and other variety hosts, who could always count on him to deliver big laughs with his "letters from Mama back in Mt. Idy" routines.

A pioneering multimedia star, Arquette did live shows, TV and radio, recycled his old routines into a best-selling book, *Letters From Mama* (the *SeinLanguage* of its time), and cut comedy records. Naturally, he wanted to sing, too. Hence this 1954 LP, a batch of "letters from Mt. Idy" set to rinky-tink accompaniment by the "Mt. Idy Symphonette," a willfully amateurish congregation that plinks away like the Hooterville Volunteer Fire Department Band on *Petticoat Junction.* Singing is not Charlie's forte, to put it kindly, but if you can get past his billy-goat bleating and innocent, twinkly-eyed delivery, you'll find some surprisingly subversive jokes here, especially for 1954. Judging by these songs, Charlie's little hometown of Mt. Idy is populated almost entirely with mental defectives, transvestites ("Ludlow Bean, chosen Queen of Winnimuck, Nevada"), alcoholics, and various other inbred lunatics, all with Kovacsian names like Byron Ogg, Wallace Swine, Elsie Krack, and Gomar Cool. Mt. Idy is no Mayberry. It's more like Twin Peaks!

"Mt. Idy Lullaby" is sung to a senile ninety-eight-year-old whose friends are coming to his birthday party in ambulances. The local college pep song is "Fight For Subnormal You." The age-old holiday traditions recalled in "Xmas In Mt. Idy" include "kissin' and dancin' and fistfights," putting kumquats in the kids' stockings, drunkenly shooting at Santa, and choking a moose for dinner. (Charlie wins extra points for calling the holiday "X-mas" throughout!) Other titles include "It's Cumquat Time In Mt. Idy," "Gomar, Come Out Of That Sewer!" and "Who'll Sign The Pardon For Wallace Swine?" As Charlie sings in the stirring town anthem, "These Are My People," the residents of Mt. Idy are truly "a sick, pitiful bunch."

This forgotten treasure proves that Cliff Arquette was no Square. Although the album was reissued in 1959 by Columbia, it's still a rarity in the cheap-o record bins. We demand a CD reissue!

Rex Reed
"Sugarfoot"
Ben Bagley's Vernon Duke Revisited
Crew Records Lp, 1977

In the 1950s, Ben Bagley was known for producing elegant musical comedy revues starring casts of fresh-faced newcomers on the New York theater scene. In 1960, with audiences dwindling, Bagley moved to the recording studio and began releasing his series of *Revisited* LPs. Each album had a different batch of Broadway stars (Jerry Orbach, Kaye Ballard, etc.) revisiting lost songs by one composer, such as Cole Porter. The series had a small but loyal audience among theater fans.

Still, it took Bagley seventeen years to convince a record company to let him revisit one of his favorite composers (and best friends), Vernon Duke. The fear was that Duke was too obscure, not to mention that his "lost" songs were not nearly so good as those of Alan Jay Lerner or Rodgers & Hart...in fact, judging from this album, they richly deserved to get lost! Perhaps that explains why this LP features the most motley assortment of alleged musical stars that ever appeared on a Ben Bagley album. It not only contains song stylings by Tammy Grimes, Anthony *Psycho* Perkins, and Joan Rivers (*see listings elsewhere*), but also includes the recording debut of famously bitchy film critic Rex Reed, who sounds as if he took singing lessons from Mae West and Raquel Welch while shooting *Myra Breckinridge* (1970).

Mercifully, Reed sings just one song, but what a doozy! "Sugarfoot," a bouncy love duet from one of Duke's countless Broadway flops (*Jackpot*, 1944), is so twee, it sounds like what someone who despises musical theater must imagine all show tunes sound like. We would say that the lyrics, by the normally reliable Howard Dietz, are idiotic, but that would be unfair to idiots. The idea is that the lovers have so many cute pet names for each other, they simply never run out, so they list a few: "My sugarfoot! My tall turtle dove!... My little dinosaurus!... My great wandering, wisteria vine!" It sounds as if Dietz just jotted down the first words that popped into his head, then went to dinner. For comparison, imagine Paul McCartney recording "Yesterday" with his original dummy lyrics, "Scrambled Eggs."

Assisted by the deadpan Blossom Dearie, with backup chirping by the notorious Keiffer Twins (singing midget sisters that Bagley stumbled upon in a nightclub in New Jersey), Reed warbles charming lines like "You're so sweet, you give a guy a toothache" in a flat, fey tenor that makes Richard Simmons sound like Howard Keel. Suddenly, we realize exactly what Tommy Tune would sound like if he were completely tone-deaf. This cut is proof that those who can't sing, teach, and those who can't be taught become critics.

All this, plus great liner notes, including a story about Reed's collection of celebrity hosiery (black opera hose with lacy garter belt labeled, gulp!... "Warren Beatty"?)! This LP, reissued in 1984 by Painted Smiles Records, is an embarrassment of riches! Buy a copy *now*!

Rona Barrett
Miss Rona Sings
Hollywood's Greatest Hits
Miss Rona Records LP, 1974

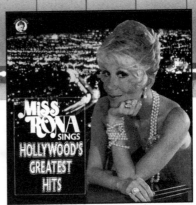

It might be hard to believe, but a scant twenty years ago, serious journalists didn't think of showbiz gossip as "real" news. They actually believed that some silly civil war in Bosnia or deadly earthquake in Swaziland was more important than some movie star getting caught in his BMW with a hooker! Today, of course, we know better. And for this advance, we owe a huge debt to that pioneer of mindless Tinseltown chatter, Rona Barrett.

After the grungy, "let it all hang out" late sixties, people were hungry for glamour. And since Hollywood hadn't had any glamour since Marilyn Monroe died, gossip columnist Rona Barrett decided to re-create it all by herself. Combining schmoozy hyperbole with catty, Brooklyn-accented smarminess, she pumped new life into the dusty old Hedda Hopper rituals: splashy movie premieres, bed-hopping stars, Liz Taylor's umpteenth divorce, etc. Rona's column was so successful, she soon began making annoying appearances on *Good Morning, America* and *Entertainment Tonight* (the first example of Hollywood puffery masquerading as news). For a while, Rona was everywhere: at every Hollywood party, in her own magazine, on all the TV talk shows. But deep down she knew she wasn't truly a star until she made her own embarrassing celebrity record.

As you might guess from the record label (Miss Rona Records), this is a vanity project, from the glamorous cover photo of our bouffanted chanteuse preening before the twinkling lights of Hollywood, right down to the back cover's jumble of off-kilter photos and mismatched typestyles. The songs are all standards from Hollywood's olden days, like "Lullabye of Broadway" and "As Time Goes By," and surprisingly, Rona sings them pretty well. She's sometimes a bit heavy on the kittenish mewling (she must've been spending a lot of time going through Diana Ross's garbage), but listening to her sing is still much more enjoyable than listening to her talk. Too bad she sinks this record by starting every song with a spoken introduction! And she can't be content just telling us the song's history. No, she has to throw in some nasty gossip, too. For instance, she introduces "Somewhere Over The Rainbow" by blabbing all the juicy details of the agonies Judy Garland endured for *The Wizard Of Oz,* such as having her teeth capped, getting trussed into a corset, and having her nostrils stuffed with cotton. Boy, Rona sure can set a mood!

In 1980, Rona signed an exclusive contract with NBC, which foisted her onto *The Tomorrow Show.* Tom Snyder refused to hide his overt disdain for her, and soon they were reporting from separate coasts, in a vain hope that placing an entire continent between the two would defuse their mutual hatred. After less than a year, Rona walked out. Her career never reached its previous heights again, but at least we have this LP...and, of course, a debased, trash tabloid culture...to remember her by.

Uri Geller
Uri Geller
Columbia Records LP, 1975

Back in the wild 1970s, psychic watch-repairman Uri Geller was *the* hot new talk show guest, what with his "psychokinetic" ability to bend spoons and house keys. So Columbia Records allowed him to try bending ears as well. Teaming up with pianist Byron Janis and composer-arranger Del Newman (who had prior experience with mushy mysticism from his work on several Cat Stevens LPs), Geller gifted his disciples with an album of swirling strings and oohing choruses, topped with his own lyrics, either sung by future disco-diva Maxine Nightingale or else recited by Uri himself in a somnambulant, high-pitched whisper, complete with thick Israeli accent.

And, oh! what lyrics they are! In the wacky world of spaced-out New Age drivel, Uri Geller makes Edie Brickell sound like Eddie Van Halen! To quote a few random phrases: "Hear, the voice, the soft enchanted voice" that "makes the flowers dream" as stars "drip of thunder colors," and "a tiny drop of tear" falls off "the eye of a molecule." This raises The Eternal Question, "What the HELL is he talking about?" That, he cannot tell you. But he can tell you how to bend spoons with your brain! And you don't even have to stick them in your ear! Just play the last track, "Mood," where listeners are urged to hold a hard object and stroke it gently as Geller softly commands, "Bend...bend..." (Warning! Male listeners *should not* practice self-abuse while listening to this cut!) Even better is the record jacket, which not only depicts Geller striding across the cosmos in maroon polyester shirt, wide belt, and burnt-orange bell bottoms, like some transdimensional Greg Brady, but which also includes a sheet of "scientific" testimonials to his powers and a disclaimer that CBS and all parties involved "take no responsibility of the experiments herein." We assume they're talking about the failed musical experiments.

Uri Geller's star dimmed somewhat after psychic skeptic James "The Amazing" Randi wrote a critical biography of Geller and began dogging his steps, imitating his effects using common household items and magic store props. But Geller still has his hardcore believers, and for them, this LP is highly recommended. For more psychic fun and games, visit Uri's "Psychic City" on the Internet at http://www.urigeller.com/ and hire him to consult your business and locate diamonds in your backyard. But don't blame us if your hard drive warps.

A postscript: While being interviewed about the *Bongos, Bass, and Bob* album, Penn Jillette of Penn & Teller enthusiastically volunteered his favorite lyric line from this LP. It appears in the song "Velvet Space," in which Uri is imagining floating through space and talking to God.

The line: "Oh, God! You're *so* big!!"

Penn & Teller
Never Mind The Sex Pistols, Here's Bongos, Bass, and Bob!
50 Skidillion Watts LP, 1988

Penn & Teller like to call themselves "a couple of eccentric guys who have learned to do a few really cool things." They ram knives through their hands, juggle broken liquor bottles, do card tricks with forklifts, and make magic look cool, despite the best efforts of David Copperfield to make it look geeky. So it's no shock that we chose their LP as the Coolest Celebrity Record Ever!

As you might expect, records are mostly Penn Jillette's department (although his silent partner, Teller, provides keyboards and backup vocals and designed the cover). Penn explained that the *Bongos, Bass, and Bob* saga began quite by accident in the late 1980s, when he founded his own label (50 Skidillion Watts Of Power In The Hands Of Babies) to put out records by two of his favorite rock artists, Half Japanese and former Velvet Underground drummer Maureen Tucker. But Maxwell's club in Hoboken refused to book his label showcase concert unless there were three bands. Not wanting to pay for a third band, Penn just called up his pals, Dean J. Seal (bongos) and Bob "Running" Elk (guitar), with whom he played bass for fun, and they performed songs they'd written while sitting around his living room. The positive reaction prompted this album, recorded in two weeks with help from more Penn pals, such as Fred Frith, Ann Magnuson, and Kramer (the Butthole Surfers' producer, *not* the *Seinfeld* guy).

The BB&B sound is unique: all mid-range (no bass drum), with quirky, catchy melodies and twisted but very funny lyrics. Among the highlights: "Oral Hygiene," a sprightly calypso toe-tapper about obsessive flossing; the hypnotic alternative radio hit, "Thorazine Shuffle"; a romantic ballad, "Clearly Unhealthy," in which Penn lists various ways he would maim himself to prove his love ("She could put Drano under my eyelids!"). The hilarious rocker, "Clothes Of The Dead," which makes wearing second-hand clothing sound like necrophilia; and Penn's brilliant portrayal of a mentally unraveling ex-boyfriend, "Gun In My Hand, And I'm Waitin' On My Woman" (note to Crispin Glover: Cover this song). Penn recalls that at one point, his album was higher on college airplay charts than Lou Reed's major label latest, "New York," which caused Reed to gripe, "I'm so happy your goddamn hobby is doing better than my career."

Penn and Kramer now have a new group called Captain Howdy, which released a great single, "Best Song In The World" b/w "Dino's Head," a ridiculously detailed, stream-of-consciousness monologue about Penn's career (his dressing room in Vegas has Dean Martin's actual shower head, thus the title). By the time this book is published, both cuts, along with lots of other cool stuff we've heard in demo form, should be out on an album, *Tattoo Of Blood* (Shimmy Disc, JAF Box 1187, New York, NY 10116). We'd say the future of celebrity records is in bloody good hands!

Crispin Hellion Glover
The Big Problem
Restless Records CD, 1989

Crispin Glover is known for three things: playing Michael J. Fox's father in *Back To The Future* (1985), portraying oddballs in quirky art films like *River's Edge* (1987), and nearly decapitating David Letterman with a poorly aimed karate kick during an incoherent, zonked-out guest shot. Recently, Glover has all but abandoned his movie career to concentrate on various avant-garde art projects such as books, a slide show, and most notorious of all, this strange, disturbing CD. (Full title: "The Big Problem ≠ The Solution. The Solution = Let It Be." Got that?)

The Big Problem is easily the weirdest celebrity record ever made, and if they have celebrity records on Mars, it's probably weirder than any of them, too. Large portions of it consist of Glover reading excerpts from *Oak Mot* and *Rat Catching,* two dreary, nineteenth-century books he republished after altering passages at random and adding his own bizarre illustrations of dead rats, disembodied hands and faces, and what appears to be a Ku Klux Klansman with antlers. Suitably surreal accompaniment for the readings, as well as the music for the original songs, is provided by producers Barnes and Barnes, creators of the Dr. Demento classic, "Fish Heads." One of the Barneses is Billy Mumy, former child star of the appropriately titled *Lost In Space,* and the cryptic liner notes also thank such stars as Nicolas Cage, Mia Sara, members of Devo, and Uma Thurman.

Our favorites among the original songs are "Clowny Clown Clown," which sounds like Dr. Seuss after a frontal lobotomy, and "Auto-Manipulator," an uproariously vulgar rap song about masturbation (it really cranks, dude!). There are also some intriguing covers. Glover portrays "The Man On The Flying Trapeze" as an evil, drooling user of women, and on "Never Say 'Never' To Always," he proves his ability as the ideal interpreter of the compositions of Charles Manson. But for sheer fun, the best track is his inside-out cover of "These Boots Are Made For Walkin'." The arrangement is similar to Nancy Sinatra's, but whereas Nancy sang it as a declaration of empowerment, Glover whines and yelps the lyrics, choking back sobs and creating a perfect portrait of a dumped loser boyfriend, impotently enraged, spewing wimpy threats from safely behind his ex's chain-link fence. If there is a thin line between brilliance and insanity, then on this cut, Crispin Glover completely erases it.

If you're daring enough to take a walk on the weird side with one of the more...shall we say, "unique"?...minds in show business, then you need this CD. If you can't find it in stores, you can order it (and keep up with all of Crispin's current doings) by phoning 213-464-5053. After you hear the CD, you can call the same number and leave a message telling Crispin what you think it all means. If you figure it out, let us know, too.

Richard Simmons
Reach
Elektra Records LP, 1982

We'd like to start off by saying some-thing nice about Richard Simmons: Sure, he's as annoying as a swarm of bees, his voice sounds like Jerry Lewis with clogged sinuses, and his gym shorts are *way* too small. But he *has* helped a lot of tragically obese people. While other TV exercise gurus got rich off narcissists longing for perfect buns, Simmons got rich by helping regular Americans (i.e., people so huge, they have their own zip codes) stop eating before they explode. For this, we salute him. Now, let's get nasty and discuss *Reach,* Simmons's weird hybrid of an aerobics record, inspirational lecture, and sensitive singer/songwriter LP.

In the pre-VCR days, exercise records were small but steady sellers. Some of the earliest were cut by health food zealot Dr. John Harvey Kellogg. For years, Debbie Drake owned the field. Then, in the eighties, Jane Fonda started a vogue for celebrity aerobics albums. (We owe our sculpted bods to the Arnold Schwarzenegger LP!) Most featured recent dance hits, with the star simply calling out the exercises and occasionally shouting, "Feel the burn!" (We always imagined them doing this from an overstuffed divan, while scarfing down Godiva chocolates.) But as usual, that gurly-man Richard Simmons had to be different! So for his first (and only) album, he decided not only to lead the exercises, but to cowrite and *sing* all the songs! See, you're sweating already!

In the liner notes, Simmons thanks all the people who helped him move from singing in the shower (boy, there's an image you don't want in your head) to singing in the studio, including his voice coach, who shall remain nameless but not blameless. The songs all have exercise-related titles ("Lift It Up," "Reach," "Stop And Start"), except Simmons wants to do more than build your body. He also seeks to enrich your soul, with lyrics like, "Any mountain you can climb, if you just make up your mind," "You're the best one to care about yourself," and our favorite, "Don't cook for two when there's only you." Simmons sings this tripe (Tripe! Yum!) in the same shrill trill he uses on Letterman's show when he sings about éclairs to the tune of "Yankee Doodle Dandy." (Believe it or not, *two* singles were released from this LP, for people who enjoy sweating on jukeboxes.) Besides singing all these generic dance/rock tunes, Simmons also shouts exercise instructions and constantly offers positive "daily affirmations." It's like being trapped in gym class at that high school from *Fame,* with today's substitute teacher, Stuart Smalley. Our advice to the overweight: Skip this and buy *Sweatin' To The Oldies,* where Simmons leaves the singing to such avatars of sensible eating as Fats Domino and Chubby Checker. Now, who's up for chili dogs!?!

Hugh Downs
An Evening With Hugh Downs
Epic Records LP, 1959

Have you ever picked up a book about television, hoping to find some funny pictures of Mr. Ed in big Bermuda shorts, only to find that it was filled with dense gobbledygook about the impact of mass media on modern society, or some such blather? If so, then it's likely you stumbled upon Marshall McLuhan's theory that television is a "cool" medium, in which laid-back, guy-next-door types can thrive for years without wearing out their welcomes, while "hot" stars with strong personalities alienate viewers quickly. This explains why Jerry Lewis is only allowed on TV once a year, on a holiday weekend when most people are at the beach anyway, while the almost pod-person-like Hugh Downs is in the *Guinness Book of Records* for logging the most hours on network commercial TV. From *Caesar's Hour* to *Concentration* to *20/20*, Downs has been puttering about on our television sets for over forty years! Apparently, a lot of people just can't get enough of Hugh Downs.

If you're one of them, then rejoice: you can buy this LP and spend *every* evening with Hugh Downs! Gaze lovingly upon the cover photo of your hero, Hugh, gently strumming his acoustic guitar by candlelight, while dressed for seduction in velour smoking jacket, starched white dress shirt, and tie! Read the copious liner notes, which detail Hugh's many accomplishments: skin diver, astronomer, antique gun and furniture authority, student of American history, mental health volunteer, composer, pianist, guitarist, artist, amateur physicist, hi-fi set builder, double-naught spy...the list goes on and on. (They forgot to mention he was the first man to discuss his hair transplant on TV, which encouraged Joey Bishop to get plugs, too!) But most wondrous of all is the record itself: a full dozen old folk songs for old folks, performed by Hugh and his magic guitar!

These aren't the folk songs of the 1960s, full of anger and turmoil. These are the really archaic folk songs, the kind that Tom Lehrer once said were so atrocious because they were written by *The People*. And Hugh knows them all: "Scarlet Ribbons," "I Wonder As I Wander," "The E-R-I-E Was A-risin'," "Drink To Me Only With Thine Eyes," and other lugubrious ballads about love, the sea, the Civil War, Jesus, and cholera epidemics. The surprise here is that Hugh isn't a bad singer. If your dad sang well enough to be allowed a solo in your church's Christmas pageant, then chances are he sounded a lot like Hugh Downs. His mellifluous baritone, while not always steady on the high notes, is at least not grating. In fact, it's so soothing that, combined with the snail's pace of most of the songs, and the occasional informative lecture Hugh tosses in on the meaning of one song or another, we just can't help falling...ZZZZzzzz...HUH?! Wha?! Oh, sorry, we dozed off for a minute! Until Marshall McLuhan records an album of lullabies, this is the next best thing to Sominex.

Mr. T (Lawrence Tureaud)
Be Somebody, Or Be Somebody's Fool
MCA Records LP, 1984

Muscled-up, medallion-encased and mohawked Mr. T started life as one of twelve siblings in a welfare family in the worst ghetto in Chicago, but rather than let his surroundings defeat him, he resolved to work extra hard to overcome them. He became Leon Spinks's bodyguard, won the America's Toughest Bouncer competition twice running, then leaped to stardom in *Rocky III* (1982). For a time in the mid-1980s, Mr. T was a true American phenomenon. Much to the consternation of TV critics, his cartoonishly violent NBC series, *The A-Team,* lodged at the top of the ratings, as did his cartoon show on Saturday mornings. Besides all the *A-Team* toys and lunch boxes, there were Mr. T dolls (sorry, "action figures"), an inspirational autobiography (*Mr. T: The Man With The Gold*), and, of course, this album.

To his credit, Mr. T was genuinely interested in helping kids. A deeply religious man despite his external bluster, he constantly visited children's hospitals and inner-city schools to deliver messages of hope and self-reliance. And he saw this album as a way to reach impressionable kids by using the hip, happenin' rap music that they loved, to deliver some positive messages. So his intentions were extremely admirable.

Still, we pity da fool who paid retail for this record! Within seconds of putting it on, Mr. T makes it painfully clear that it's not just white men who can't rap. Despite the expert guidance of the "Associate Producer for Mr. T's Vocal" (that original gangsta himself, Ice-T, in an early, embarrassing gig that he probably doesn't want his gangsta posse to know about), Mr. T proves to be about as graceful and fluid at rapping as he would be at toe dancing. He barks each word like an angry pit bull, trying desperately to keep up with the music, and it sounds as if he's reading the lyrics off the world's slowest TelePrompTer: "If ya wanna be COOL!...Jus' like ME!...You bettah TRY!...Real HARD!....To!....BE!.....Some!.....BAH!........Dee!" You can practically hear Ice-T pounding him on the shoulder with his fist to help him find the beat. Combine this with the wimpy pop-disco arrangements, children's choruses (ARRRRGHH!), and general slipshod production values (the dorky cover shot, the three different vocal credits for a track that turns out to be instrumental), and poor Ice-T must've been thinking, "This is the last time I help Cousin Mr. just because he's a member of the T family! At least Uncle Booker was smart enough to say no!" If you enjoy this record, you are a true masochist, and you will also want to hunt up the companion home video. It gives you a good idea of what an *ABC After School Special* would look like in the Twilight Zone.

Cybill Shepherd
Does It...To Cole Porter
Paramount Records LP, 1974

Besides Bette Davis, few actresses have been so completely convinced that they were *really* born to sing as Cybill Shepherd, or caused more suffering, monetary loss, and career destruction trying to prove it. Over several albums, numerous television appearances, nightclub tours, and one fifty-megaton bomb of a movie musical, Cybill has warbled relentlessly on, like a losing contestant in the Miss Teenage America pageant (which she was) trying desperately to make us think she is Sarah Vaughan (which she ain't).

Cybill Does It...To Cole Porter (and boy, does she!) was Cybill's debut LP, and like all her early film work, owes its existence to her then paramour, movie director Peter Bogdanovich. He produced (and "directed," whatever that means) this album, which combined his two obsessions: recycling showbiz genres of the past, and turning his fashion model girlfriend into a star. The bedazzled Bogdanovich, like John Lennon before him, proved that love is not merely blind, it is also quite tone-deaf. He never even noticed that Cybill's singing, while hardly horrible, is extremely variable. Just as you're marveling that she was able to accomplish a rather nifty trill, you notice that she's just gone slightly off pitch. Then she ends the line on a note so flat, you'd swear she ran over it with a steamroller.

This LP was the precursor to *At Long Last Love* (1975), a movie which also prompted plenty of cursing. Bogdanovich tried to use Cole Porter's music to lend both projects a veneer of class they would otherwise never merit. Yet even this feeble stab at sophistication is undermined by the album's adolescent smuttiness. To attract swingin' seventies record buyers, Peter and Cybill chose nothing but songs about sex ("Let's Do It," "Let's Misbehave") and panted that they were the original, "unexpurgated" versions. The lyrics never go beyond mildly naughty, but Cybill growls, sighs, and coos them like a phone sex operator working on commission. Still, this LP is a must for bad-movie buffs, because it demonstrates the one way that "At Long Last Love" could've been even worse, and that's if Bogdanovich had carried out his original plan to costar in it himself! If you think Burt Reynolds was no Fred Astaire, then wait'll you hear Petey duet with songbird Cybill on "In The Morning, No." (It pops up *five times*, and will have you screaming "No!" all day long, as well.) He sounds like exactly what he is: a nerdy ex-film critic with delusions of musical talent (*see "Rex Reed"*).

Too bad our two sex-crazed egotists never took lessons in class from the Old Master, Cary Grant, who was obviously pressured for a cover blurb. With tongue firmly in cheek, Grant offered this simple, yet eloquent, backhanded compliment: "I only wish Cole could have heard it!"

Bruce Willis
The Return Of Bruno
Motown Records CD, 1987

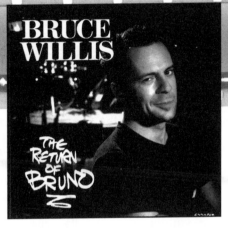

When Bruce Willis did his frat-boy soul singer imitation in his popular Seagram's wine cooler commercials of the mid-1980s, fans laughed at his smug audaciousness and bought the wine coolers by the case. The success of this ironic joke convinced some misled soul at Motown, who clearly should have known better, that Willis was a genuine crooner, and he was quickly signed to a multi-album deal reported to be among the richest in Motown history.

Imagine the egg on Berry Gordy's face when Willis delivered this limp performance-art experiment. Not content with merely doing a goofy imitation of a soul singer, Bruce created a whole new persona (the hard-partying lounge singer, "Bruno," sort of a forgotten Blues Brother by way of Spinal Tap) and performed all the songs in character. So now we had a smirking actor *pretending* he was a smirking, second-rate R&B singer *pretending* to imitate real soul singers! You couldn't cut through all the irony with a blow-torch. Naturally, "Bruno" was bigger than a mere LP: the project included a cable TV special, talk show appearances, magazine covers, star-studded club dates, and all the other elephantine hype that accompanies modern, megabuck Hollywood deals masquerading as art.

And what was all the hoopla about? A messy *Hudson Hawk* of an album that alternates between pale copies of JB's and Bar-Kays soul riffs ("Comin' Right Up," "Jackpot") and limp retreads of fifties and sixties classics, such as "Young Blood" and "Secret Agent Man." In addition to bad singing, Die-Hard party machine Willis also contributes hyperactive harmonica solos with an artistic virtuosity that makes Dan Aykroyd sound like Charlie Musselwhite. He simply blows as hard as he can while shaking his head violently from side to side, sounding like Katharine Hepburn with a harmonica stuck in her throat. The liner notes credit both a doctor and a nurse; perhaps they were there to administer the Heimlich maneuver after each harmonica solo.

This LP proved conclusively that while Bruce Willis could be hilarious ripping through "Good Lovin'" in Shakespearean garb on *Moonlighting*, he is simply not a real singer. Compare his grunting rendition of "Under The Boardwalk" with the Drifters' magnificent original. When the lyric sheet says, "Repeat Chorus," you'll find yourself muttering, "Must we?" Amazingly, Bruce's version of "Respect Yourself" made it to number five on the *Billboard* Top 40 charts, while the Staple Singers' original only hit number twelve. Man, we must've been drinking a lot of wine coolers back in 1987!

Those who can't get enough of Bruce Willis can also pick up the soundtracks of *Moonlighting* and *Hudson Hawk*, and his solo LPs, *Heart Of Soul* (Columbia, 1990) and the highly debatable *If It Don't Kill You, It Just Makes You Stronger* (Motown, 1989).

Sid Caesar, Carl Reiner, and Howie Morris
"Goin' Crazy" b/w "You Are So Rare To Me"
RCA Records 45, 1955

In the 1950s, the talentless bums who made that noise called "rock 'n' roll" were irresistible targets for satire. And the three greatest satirists of that era all skewered them: Stan Freberg on record, *Mad* magazine in print, and Sid Caesar and his astonishing cast of costars (Imogene Coca, Carl Reiner, Howard Morris) and writers (Woody Allen, Neil Simon, Larry Gelbart, Mel Brooks) on TV.

Besides being one of the greatest sketch comics ever, Sid Caesar was also a talented musician. His earliest ambition was to be a saxophone player, and his first acting job was pretending to be a student so he could sneak into classes at Juilliard. He eventually played sax with several big bands and recorded with the Shep Fields Orchestra. Naturally, he was contemptuous of the simple chords, thumping beats, and off-key harmonies of fifties rock, so he took revenge during the 1956-57 run of *Caesar's Hour* on NBC with "The Three Haircuts." This running sketch was a parody of hyperactive vocal groups like the Crew Cuts and the Diamonds. The Haircuts were Caesar, Reiner, and Morris, all decked out in matching loud jackets and sky-high pompadour wigs. Their songs weren't even scripted: Caesar recalls that the three would just run onstage as the band played, wiggle and gyrate their pelvises (never in synch), and shout anything that came into their heads, usually something brilliant like "Oh, baby, baby, baby!" It was utter chaos, and it always brought down the house.

Deprived of their visual element for this 45, the Haircuts were forced to discipline themselves and sing the same words at the same time (but not in the same key: then they wouldn't sound like the Crew Cuts!). "Goin' Crazy" begins with Caesar smugly announcing, "This side of the record outsold the other side, three to one!" They then launch into an upbeat rhythm number whose lyrics consist solely of the phrase "Goin' crazy! Doodle-loop-doo-doo-doo!" repeated for two minutes, ending on a big crescendo: "Over YOOOOOOOU!" Ta-daaa! Caesar begins the flip side, "You Are So Rare To Me," by introducing the group (Pete, Alk, and Mike Haircut) and declaring, "We cut this record last night at a party, just for kicks! It's already gone over the seven million mark...and it hasn't even been released yet!" The song is a parody of the overwrought ballads of Johnny Ray, with each separate word shouted at the very tops of their lungs: "YOU! ARE! SO! RAAAARE! To MEEEEE!...SO! VEH! REE! RAAAARE! To MEEEEE!..." After repeating this a few times, they offer a hiccup solo, then the denouement: "WON'T! YOU! BEEE! RAAAAAARE?!" No wonder Johnny Ray went deaf. If any record company executives are reading this, we'd like to point out that if Caesar, Reiner, and Morris are all still willing, Michael Bolton is simply CRYING OUT to be "saluted" by The Three Haircuts.

Honor Blackman and Patrick Macnee
"Kinky Boots"
Decca Records UK 45, 1964

PATRICK MACNEE & HONOR BLACKMAN

The Avengers is fondly remembered by Americans as a witty spy series from the mid-1960s, starring the delectable Diana Rigg and the unflappable Patrick Macnee. But in fact, by the time ABC picked it up in 1966, it had already been a huge hit in Britain for five years, where it made an overnight star of Macnee's original partner, the tight leather-clad, motorcycle-riding blonde, Honor Blackman. The show's popularity gave rise to an almost Beatlesque level of merchandising in the U.K., including dolls, jigsaw puzzles, games, models of Mr. Steed's 1929 Bentley, the "John Steed Swordstick" toy (a plastic walking stick/sword combo which also functioned as a water pistol), an Avengers essay contest sponsored by a pet food maker, and fashion lines for both men and women, no doubt inspired by the footwear fad Blackman set off with her penchant for high leather boots.

By 1964, the high boot craze was so widespread, half the women in Britain were clomping about as if they were just back from the trout stream. So Blackman and Macnee were hustled into the studio to cut a song about it, thereby managing the neat trick of merchandising their reaction to their own merchandising. The result was the insidious "Kinky Boots," one of those maddeningly simple, English music-hall ditties that lodge in your head and perk cheerfully along like a happy little coffeepot for hours on end, until you just want to kill yourself.

Musically, "Kinky Boots" isn't much more than "Shave and a haircut! Two bits!" repeated ad nauseum. Lyrically, it has Blackman and Macnee taking turns listing all the kinds of boots that those mindless gals are buying up: low boots, high boots, patent leather thigh boots (toot-toot!), round boots, black boots...every boot shy of Clint Eastwood snake stompers gets a mention. Then they list all the different types of silly women who are wearing them: square girls, cool girls, "sexy little schoolgirls" (Macnee brings a disturbing enthusiasm to his reading of that line), sweet girls, street girls (toot-toot!), and so on. To add that extra little edge of annoyance, Macnee is always about half a beat behind and hurrying to catch up to the music. The first time you hear this record, you'll say we're overreacting. You might even think it's cute. The third time you play it, you'll start to see our point. After five plays, you'll want to call the Avengers and sic them on the songwriters. And when you realize it's now stuck in your brain on permanent replay, you'll want to pull on your kinky boots and personally stomp every last copy into little vinyl shards! But that won't be easy, because this 45 has been reissued twice!

By dropping out of The Avengers when she did, Honor Blackman saved America from the "kinky boots" craze and from this record. But she did go on to play Pussy Galore in Goldfinger (1964), and so can make some tenuous claim to helping set off the sexual revolution.

And Just To Be Fair...
Some Singers Who Shouldn't Act

We'd hate for you to think we do nothing with our lives but make fun of actors who can't sing. We also make fun of singers who can't act! In the interest of fair play, here is a by-no-means complete list of these budding thespians, along with some movies they should have passed on...

Tony Bennett *The Oscar* (1965)
If only for the immortal line "Here you sit, Frankie, on top of a glass mountain CALLED success!"

Diana Ross *Mahogany* (1975)
Do you know where you're goin' to? Not to the Oscars!

Conway Twitty *College Confidential* (1960)
Conway portrays a member of a student body filled with angst over an allegation that professor Steve Allen owns a stag movie.

Paul McCartney *Give My Regards To Broad Street* (1984)
Where the lost tapes were (unfortunately) found.

Paul Simon *One Trick Pony* (1980)
Somehow, Paul plays a washed-up, sixties pop star unconvincingly.

The Village People *Can't Stop The Music* (1980)
It not only stopped the music, it killed their careers.

Elvis Presley - Everything after *King Creole* (1958)
One song says it all: "No Room To Rhumba In A Sports Car."

Nancy Sinatra *Speedway* (with Elvis, 1968)
These ~~boobs~~ boots do all my acting.

Bob Geldof *Pink Floyd: The Wall* (1980)
Mind-numbing portrait of the self-pitying rock star as Führer.

Prince *Under The Cherry Moon* (1986)
Where Vanity got the better of him.

Bob Dylan *Hearts Of Fire* (with Fionna, 1987)
Bob needs subtitles, and he's (supposedly) speaking English.

Neil Sedaka *The Playgirl Killer,* aka *Decoy For Terror* (1970)
Psychotic murderer pursued by Sedaka in a bathing suit.

Mick Jagger *Performance* (1968)
Jagger stretches his abilities to play a creepy, decadent rock star.

Roger Daltrey, Rick Wakeman *Lisztomania* (1975)
Ken Russell, ten-foot penis, pissing scene. It's a musical!

Harry Nilsson, Ringo Starr *Son Of Dracula* (1974)
This Dracula really sucks, but died easier than most.

Sting *Dune* (1984) or *The Bride* (1985)
In both cases, he created a monster.

Hank Williams, Jr. *A Time To Sing* (1968)
And you thought Kawlija was a wooden Indian!

Mama Cass Elliot *Pufnstuf* (1970)
And stuff, and stuff, and stuff...

Chynna Phillips *The Invisible Kid* (1988)
Secret formula leads kid straight to girls' locker room. Zowie!

Mel Tormé, Paul Anka *Girl's Town* (with Mamie Van Doren, 1959)
So brilliant, cast reunited for *Private Lives Of Adam & Eve* (1960)

Peter Frampton *Sgt. Pepper's Lonely Hearts Club Band* (1978)
Cinematic neutron bomb. Only the big cheeseburger was left standing.

Yoko Ono *Satan's Bed* (1965)
Yoko is kidnapped by murderous gang and screams her way out.

Roy Orbison *The Fastest Guitar Alive* (1968)
The guitar is a gun, get it? Like *The Wild, Wild West* with shades.

Sonny Bono *Troll* (1986)
He didn't play the title role, they wanted a bigger star.

Cyndi Lauper *Vibes* (1988)
Plays a psychic who should have known this was a train wreck.

KISS *KISS Meets The Phantom Of The Park* (1978)
We are powahful supah-bein's from da far-flung galaxy uh Brooklyn!

Kenny Rogers *Six Pack* (1982)
His first film. Should have known when to fold 'em.

Courtney Love *Straight To Hell* (1987)
The lead's whining girlfriend; Courtney's first shot at fame misses.

Olivia Newton-John *Two Of A Kind* (with John Travolta, 1983)
Duo forestall God's destruction of the world but not their careers.

David Johansen (Buster Poindexter) *Car 54, Where Are You?* (1992)
Oooh! Oooh! This script stinks.

Grace Jones *Conan The Destroyer* (1984)
Makes small leap from "Nightclubbing" to clubbing everyone in sight.

Chuck Berry *American Hot Wax* (1978)
Sure, Chuck! We BELIEVE you'd play a concert without being paid!

Ferlin Husky *Hillbillies In A Haunted House* (1967)
Las Vegas Hillbillies gambled on sequel and lost again.

Luciano Pavarotti *Yes, Giorgio* (1982)
No, Luciano! Best part? "...where leetle kebble cars, climb halfway to..."

Alice Cooper *Sextette* (1978)
Alice sings a disco song in a tux to eighty-six-year-old Mae West. Yow!

Johnny Cash *Door-To-Door Maniac* (with Merle Travis, 1965)
"Hello, I'm Johnny Cash. Prepare to DIE!!"

Neil Diamond *The Jazz Singer* (1980)
Had opportunity to hide behind black face, but his ego won out.

Susanna Hoffs *The Allnighter* (1987)
Only rock singer nude scene to be directed by the star's mother.

Madonna *Shanghai Surprise* (1986), *Who's That Girl* (1987),
Bloodhounds of Broadway (1989), *Body Of Evidence* (1993)...
Say, maybe we should have named this page after her!

Hollywood Hi·Fi Video Companion

Some celebrity musical performances are more easily available on video than on record. Next time everything good is gone from the video store, and you're desperate for a cheap laugh at some big shot's expense, try these.

Cynthia (1947),* in which MGM forced fifteen-year-old Elizabeth Taylor to make her singing debut, and she turned out to sound like Disney's Snow White with an ear infection. Thirty years passed before she dared to sing again for *The Blue Bird* (1976) and *A Little Night Music* (1978), in which she squeak-whispered "Send In The Clowns" like Judy Collins with bronchitis.

Idiot's Delight (1939),* featuring Clark Gable's oddly enjoyable hambone tap dance to "Puttin' On The Ritz."

Riders Of Destiny (1933), *The Man From Utah* (1934), *Westward Ho* and *The Lawless Range* (1935), all starring a young John Wayne as "Singin' Sandy," a lawman who warbles western tunes a cappella as he moseys t'wards a shoot out. He may have been dubbed by Smith Ballew or Glenn Strange, but if so, they sounded just as flat and tuneless as you'd imagine the Duke would.

Hollywood Revue of 1929,* the most hilarious of several early talkies in which former chorus girl Joan Crawford shows off her unique "vivacious musical talents." Joan's singing is inept enough, but she also tap dances like a hippo trying to stomp out a grease fire. (Don't be fooled by her on-key, yet terrifying, blackface rendition of "Two-Faced Woman" in 1953's *Torch Song*. She lip-synched to a vocal by India Adams.)

Born To Dance (1936),* in which Jimmy Stewart tootles "Easy To Love" in a voice that sounds like a whining collie. He was asked to sing again in *The Magic Of Lassie* (1978), probably just to keep the collie company.

Satisfaction (1988), In which *Family Ties'* Justine Bateman answers the musical question "What if Phyllis Diller had a garage band?" There is a soundtrack LP, but you must *see* this tub of offal to believe it. With Julia Roberts as the slutty drummer!

Rover Dangerfield (1991), an animated feature with Rodney Dangerfield as the voice of an incontinent dog who shows his respect for the holiest of all holidays by singing the timeless carol "I'll Never Do It On A Christmas Tree." However, he did piddle on "Twist & Shout" in *Back To School* (1986).

Finally, if all these are checked out, turn on your TV and do a little boot-scootin' to the opening theme to **Walker, Texas Ranger,** as crooned by that ass-kickin' cowboy, Chuck Norris. Now, *that's* entertainment!

* Excerpts appear in the compilation film *That's Entertainment*.

Pat Reeder has been a radio DJ and production director, commercial copywriter, and music librarian for one of America's largest radio production companies. He has also written comedy material for a number of top stars. He is a movie and theater buff and columnist for *Skeptical Briefs* magazine. Reeder and wife, Laura Ainsworth, live in a restored, turn-of-the-century house full of squawking parrots. Despite this, they somehow manage to write the daily topical comedy service "The Comedy Wire," used by radio DJs nationwide.

George Gimarc is a former DJ and programmer for several Dallas area radio stations and was among the first to torture his listeners with punk rock records back in 1977. He's written the definitive history of the U.K. punk boom (*Punk Diary 1970-1979*, St. Martin's Press) and is presently working with music legend John Lydon on the *Rotten Day* syndicated radio program. As a music archivist with a fascination for popular (and unpopular) music from the 1920s to the present, he has amassed an embarrassment of vinyl in his bulging Dallas residence, where most of the records in this book reside.

You can contact Pat and George through P.O. Box 280173, Dallas, TX 75228 or through the all-powerful and futuristic Internet at gimarc@onramp.net or poke around our site at http://www.onramp.net/RGP/Hollywood.html.

Pat & George would like to thank the following companies for making the wonderful records that we've pictured in this book. We highly recommend you buy each and every record included here, really!

A&M Records: 28, 66; ABC Paramount: 73, 106; Atlantic Records: 47; Audio Fidelity Records: 40; AZ Records: 102; Bell Records: 84; Ben Berry & Associates: 98, BLD/GS Records: 14; Brunswick: 25; Buddah Records: 19; Cameo Records: 74; Capitol Records: 17, 22, 33, 35, 50, 95; Casablanca Records: 46, 110; Chelsea Records: 85; Colgems Records: 49; Decca Records: 11, 15, 90; Del Fi Records: 45; Disneyland and Vista Records: 20, 83; Dot Records: 53, 91, 104; Elektra Records: 117; Eva Records: 34; G.N.P./Crescendo Records Co. Inc. Hollywood, CA.: 21, 92; GLW Records: 93; Infinite Visions CDs: 93; Ken Records: 79; Legend Records: 100; Liberty Records: 43, 44; MCA Records: 16, 23, 109, 119; Miss Rona Records: 113; Motown Record Company, L.P.: 121; Nashwood Records: 31; Paramount Records: 80, 120; Phonogram Records: 18, 52, 76, 82, 86,107,123; Platypus Records: 56; RCA Records: 8, 27, 39, 48, 54, 70, 105, 122; Butch Patrick aka Eddie & The Monsters 63; Restless Records: 116; Rhino Video: 97; Roulette Records: 24; United Artists Records: 94; Vee Jay Records: 59; the incomparable Penn & Teller: 115, the Mamie Van Doren archives: 101; and of course the fab Howard Frank Photo Archive, P.O. Box 50, Midwood Station, Brooklyn NY 11230: 12, 26, 29, 38, 41, 51, 60, 61, 62, 64, 67, 68, 72, 75, 78, 99, 112.

NOW YOU CAN HEAR SOME OF THE WONDERS YOU'VE READ ABOUT IN HOLLYWOOD HI-FI ON THIS FAB CD COLLECTION!

All tracks on this collection have been lovingly re-mastered from original sources in *Howl-o-Phonic Stereo-monic* sound.

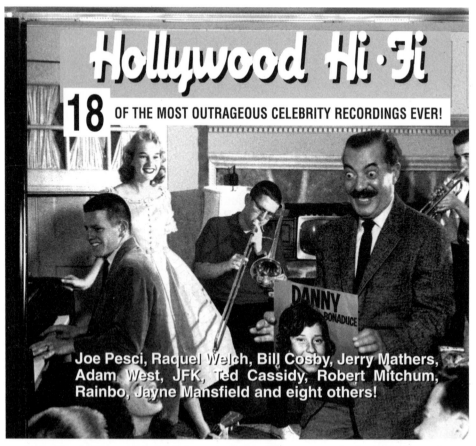

Available everywhere on Brunswick Records

BRU 81013-2